Archangel Clearings®

A Manual to Release Unwanted Energies

by

Diana Burney

TELEMACHUS PRESS

ARCHANGEL CLEARINGS®:
A MANUAL TO RELEASE UNWANTED ENERGIES

Cover art:
The Archangel photo by LJ Zinkand

Published by Telemachus Press, LLC
7652 Sawmill Road
Suite 304
Dublin, Ohio 43016
http://www.telemachuspress.com

Visit the author website:
http://www.earthrelease.com

ISBN: 978-1-7332901-0-4 (eBook)
ISBN: 978-1-7332901-1-1 (Paperback)
ISBN: 978-1-7332901-2-8 (Paperback, Spanish)

Version 2019.10.16

To my sister, Kristy

Contents

Diffusing Political Conflicts

Eradicating Social Issues

Preserving the Rainforests

Protecting Endangered Species and Other Animals

Preserving the Oceans and all Bodies of Water

Liberating Earthbound Spirits

Assisting Transitioning Souls

Foreword

It was in September 2005 when I lovingly and courageously embraced a leap of faith, and some might say "took leave of my senses," and walked away from the corporate world. Over many years that environment had offered me countless, blessed opportunities to enJOY a very comfortable existence, and extensive travel around the world—to pursue my "Higher Calling" of BEing a full time Spiritualist; Psychic/Astrologer and Medium.

I had always been aware of the importance of asking and working with Spirit for protection against the influences of all negative forces as well as BEing diligently dedicated to maintaining a clear Energy Field (Aura) and BEing grounded, specifically with the energy of our Earth. It was not until fall 2014 when I was introduced to Diana Burney's progressive, insightful and abundantly informative—and certainly most necessary—information in her first book, *Spiritual Clearings*. A few years later, with her second book, *Spiritual Balancing*, I became fully aware of the gravity of the importance of the information of Spiritual fortification for oneself as well as home and business protection and clearings.

We, Humanity, are undeniably living in the most unprecedented times of our Creative, Human Evolution. We are inundated daily with a gamut of negative influences from the overwhelming presence of electric and magnetic fields (EMFs) and the electronics we feel we cannot live without. We are also drowning in a devastating amount of erratic information and misinformation through various media sources, much of which has been designed to derail Humanity from recognizing the blessings of these unparalleled times. Simply stated, we need to embrace the awareness of the full recognition of our greatest, Human Potential.

And, in order for Humanity to be clear as to what we are BEing shown by Spirit and the Blessings at hand, we must BE clear in our BEing and grounded with the energies of our Earth, not to mention the beauty of enJOYing a peaceful and energetically balanced home environment. Through the information in Ms. Burney's first book, *Spiritual Clearings*, as well as the revered wisdom in her second book, *Spiritual Balancing*, we are offered invaluable information, illustrated in simple, loving expressions, as to how we may facilitate the process of infusing and creating clarity, balance, harmony and peacefulness in our daily lives. And now we have a complete, sacred trinity with *Archangel Clearings*!

Ms. Burney herself will state that this information is *not new* and has been available for Humanity since the dawn of time. Our great ancestors understood the importance of working with Spirit while in Human form, and how meditation and prayer—which I understand to BE one and the same—are instrumental and necessary tools on this Human Journey. The importance of energetic, self-clearings, as well as communing with Nature, have been a meaningful part of the daily spiritual maintenance of indigenous cultures such as the Native American Indians. We have not been taught in conventional education systems about the importance of these elements, and this unconventional information has been deemed as taboo—which is another ploy of the shadow forces keeping Humanity from the realization and awareness of its full potential.

Sadly, "The Powers That Be" have set out to keep this information hidden so as to maintain their *power and control* over the people. As we swiftly advance towards the *New Age*, the times of *power over* and *suppression of the masses* is coming to an end. The information in Ms. Burney's books discusses how we may, during these most extraordinary times of our Human, Creative

Evolution, *BE in the world and not of it*, and fully enJOY this most Blessed experience.

In order for us to heal our World, we must FIRST heal ourselves! As *Mahatma Gandhi* stated, we must BE the change we wish to see in the World. And, by BEing clear in our BEing, grounded with the energies of our Earth, peaceful within ourselves and enJOYing a daily existence of harmony, balance and abundance, we, by osmosis, bring to form these virtues in our world.

Archangel Clearings moves several steps further and adds to the information Ms. Burney presented in her first two highly progressive works on how to clear ourselves on a personal level, as well as how to energetically clear our homes and businesses. The book offers insight using the tools of dowsing, as well as techniques to employ for clearing our beloved pets and our cherished planet!

Since the inception of time, Spirit has lovingly shared with us this ancient wisdom, and now Ms. Burney has tirelessly and boldly allowed herself to be the conduit in bringing to form this knowledge for those who choose to receive these sacred insights. Trust in the Knowing that there is no accident that you are holding this revered information in your hands. Herein lie the tools that potentially allow you to BE acutely aware of some of the most auspicious blessings of these unprecedented times as well as the knowing of your greatest potential through these clearing processes.

Ray Sette, author, *The Planets Align So Rare: Twelve Dimensions To The Human Potential.*

August 7, 2019 *Lions Gate Portal*

Archangel Clearings®
A Manual to Release Unwanted Energies

Introduction

In the twelve years since I wrote my first book, the world has become exceedingly complicated, stressful, and unsettling. As old paradigms surface from the depths of our societies, people feel unsure, vulnerable, and confused. I was guided to write this third book to present hope, self-empowerment, a different perspective, and to provide tools for instilling and maintaining harmony and balance. Since humanity reached critical mass in March of 2017, we must help lift Mother Earth and her inhabitants to the next level toward Unity Consciousness. This upliftment is a process that can be accomplished one person at a time.

Due to the turbulence of the ongoing changes, many kinds of accumulated and trapped negative energies are being freed from the Earth. These atmospheric upheavals are assisting Mother Earth by cleansing a multitude of destructive thought forms and energies that have been anchored on, and within, the earth for centuries. The result of this natural disaster, predicted by many ancient cultures, will allow the Earth to become purified from the dense energy forms that have been attached to Her from the beginning of time.

Once these energies are released from the confines of the Earth, they become free to latch onto similar dense vibrations of others, much like the roaming of free radicals within the human body. Negative energy is produced with negative thoughts and perceptions. These toxic thought forms can cling to us when we are around exceptionally negative people or if we've been through a traumatic event. This heavy toxic energy can affect our lives by creating a barrier around us, causing us to lose faith and resist feelings of love. As a result, people can feel spiritually depleted. The Law of Attraction states that "like attracts like." This means that what you think about is what your energy field is emitting and encompasses what, ultimately, you will magnetize into your life.

The negative energies, through their attachment to individuals or things, will continue to create density and oppression. We, as individual emissaries of Light, have a responsibility to assist the Earth with this purging of negativity. The healing of this beautiful planet begins with each of us one person at a time.

The information in this book is not new. Instead, it contains ancient wisdom from various sources and spiritual teachers who assisted me with my spiritual journey over three decades. Since God has many names in different religions and cultures, I have chosen to replace the word "God" with a universal description of "Source of All There Is." I shortened that phrase to the single word "Source." Readers can insert the Divine name that is comfortable for them.

In this book there are steps that will assist in revising, re-evaluating, or re-adjusting your beliefs, values, and attitudes. Merely reading the steps is insufficient for fostering changes. Daily and consistent application of these techniques, and prayers is required. Choose a few to start and end your day. Then choose several others to weave into the fabric of your daily life. We teach people how to treat us, so be kind to others. Think before you speak, avoiding judgments. Send love to others, help people just because you can, send love daily to the animals, the oceans, the forests, and to Mother Nature. End your day with gratitude for all that you experienced and accomplished and not for what was left unfinished. Greet each new day with joy for creating something brand new.

When things around you seem to be falling apart, and you feel as if you are powerless, that is the time to tap into your spirituality. This inner focus can be accomplished through prayer, meditation, spiritual music, journaling, self-love, inspirational reading, connecting with angels and guides of the highest vibration—and by performing an Archangel Clearing.

Every day try to make a difference for someone else without being asked. See the glory in the colors and the world around you. Choose to be out in Nature as often as possible. Be mindful while eating and avoid eating meals while watching violence or listening to the news. Spend at least 10 to 15 minutes a day in silence and gratitude for what is available to you. Read something uplifting to begin and end your day. Remember that you are a spiritual Being having a human experience. Take care of your body as it's the only place where you can live. I offer this book in a spirit of sharing.

Chapter One
What is a Remote Clearing?

Since all Archangel Clearings are only performed remotely, I wanted to define how that works. Just like bacteria, that cannot be discerned physically without technology, so does the world of energy exist. A remote clearing is similar to a distant healing. The latter is also referred to as absent healing, long distance healing, or distant healing. All of these modalities consist of sending healing energy, through intention, to someone who is not physically present. It can also mean the sending, by intention, of positive psychic energy without an individual being aware that it is occurring. These methods are implemented through visualization and focus while in a meditative state, as is the Archangel Clearing Technique. A remote clearing functions in the same manner as does the scientifically proven method of prayer. Remote clearings are also effective with animals, locations, and Earth.

The reason this process can only be performed on a remote basis is that the Archangel Clearings take place in the higher realms and not on the third-dimensional level. As a general spiritual rule, nobody can receive an Archangel Clearing, or absent healing from the Archangels, without agreeing to it beforehand. Since everybody on the planet has free will, a person cannot make another individual better against that individual's will. Often some part of that individual will be angry if it happens without his or her consent. If we communicate with the person we intend to work with, and they have verbally agreed to, or requested, an Archangel Clearing, then all is well to proceed.

The Archangels have long volunteered to help humanity lift away the layers of unseen negativity that have accumulated on the Earth plane from many sources, including wars and cataclysms. Working in tandem with the Archangels and Ascended Beings is central to Archangel Clearings. The facilitator is given information in the session that might not be obtained, otherwise and the receiver is healed at a level beyond the physical realm.

The Archangel Clearings are accomplished from the spiritual body levels and then brought into consciousness through the throat, brow, crown, and heart chakras. The throat is the energy center of the first spiritual auric level. Since the throat chakra is the center of empathy, telepathy, and communication, all steps in the Archangel Clearings Technique are always spoken verbally.

The Archangels and other members of the Spiritual Clearing Team come to us from a place of great love, and offer their help in that Light. Time does not exist in the nonphysical body, and this can be used to great advantage in the Archangel Clearings Technique. What may seem impossible on the Earth level can happen readily in a remote session, and the healing can change the physical body of the person or animal or even the planet.

Asking permission to perform a remote Archangel Clearing is paramount to this process, even if consent has previously been obtained on the physical level. Receiving this permission is also just as essential to obtain from the Higher Self of infants, pets, and others who are unable to directly tell us as it is to obtain permission from conscious and aware adults.

In this time of intense Earth changes, people, animals, and the planet all need healing to a different extent. Archangel Clearings are a way to do this, and many are required to learn and practice these teachings now. Since you are reading this book, you have answered this call.

Chapter Two
Archangel Clearings

The steps to spiritual self-empowerment are many, touching every aspect of your life on the physical plane and influencing your access to the spiritual realms. One step that is essential for spiritual growth is developing the ability to remove obstacles as you journey along your path. These obstacles can be your issues, limiting beliefs, fears, and resistance. At the same time, your obstacles can be directed toward you by those energies not-of-the-Light, whose intention is to thwart any consistency and progress you might develop through your spiritual practices. Frequently, people send negative energy to others and do not mean to do it intentionally. On the other hand, many people <u>do</u> focus direct negativity toward others. Either way, the energies can back up your auric fields and create disturbances and blocks in your everyday life.

While it is beyond the scope of this book to discuss removing all self-imposed interferences, I will share some exercises and techniques that may assist you in these endeavors. I have used these techniques myself and with others, so I am aware first-hand of their benefits. My primary focus is to relay to you a process that has become my life's work. This process has been developed through dedication, willpower, perseverance, faith, trust and the strong desire to serve God, assist humanity, and heal the Earth.

Now, after 28 years performing Spiritual Clearings worldwide, I am sharing the process of Archangel Clearings® (that I trademarked) to enable others to perform Spiritual Clearings for their family members and others. The actual procedural techniques are quite comprehensive and are best shared by those who are motivated to serve the planet during their Earth sojourn. For now, the following shortened and simplified version will allow you to create a vortex of divine energy. This process will hasten your spiritual growth, enable you to awaken your spiritual gifts, increase your vibratory rate, and provide spiritual protection for your family and friends.

This Archangel Clearing Technique (ACT) is a specific procedure for removing negativity with the assistance of the seven Archangels: Michael, Rafael, Uriel, Gabriel, Jophiel, Zadkiel, Chamuel, and other highly evolved spiritual beings from the higher realms of existence. With this divine guidance, a strong vortex of energy is created through prayers, mantras, and decrees.

Through the years, I have discovered that there are many levels of negative energy in the lower and higher astral planes. Each of these categories of energy must be removed separately using the unique method and spiritual assistance for that particular level. Every person and property that receives an Archangel Clearing is helped to the maximum extent with permission from the Universe to avoid karmic disruption.

A combination of short and long-term benefits develops as a direct result of the implementation of an Archangel Clearing. The process is only performed remotely, and it removes discordant energies from a person or an environment through a process of focus and intention, with spiritual support.

Typically, there is a remarkable positive change in the person, animal, or environment within 72 hours after the Clearing is performed. However, this Archangel Clearing process is not a panacea, and daily "maintenance" must be provided after the Archangel Clearing is completed. Personal boundaries of those performing Archangel Clearings need to be established and reinforced. The aura needs to be fortified, and thoughts, habits, and belief systems must be evaluated, and often changed.

After an Archangel Clearing, individuals experience a restoration period over several months. During this time, the body is rejuvenating spiritually, adjusting to a higher energy level and establishing a new healthy pattern. This restoration period is similar to programming a computer and is helped by prayers, meditation, conscious language, affirmations, and daily spiritual practice.

The success of an Archangel Clearing for an individual depends on a person's willingness to change his/her thoughts, actions, and habits to affect permanent change. If a person goes back to old destructive ways, more negative energies will return. However; when an individual does commit to change, the path of choice is awakened through free will and one's spiritual journey.

Situations that May Require a Personal Archangel Clearing

LIFE EXPERIENCES
- History of severe illness, hospitalization or surgery
- Childhood injury or difficult birth
- Addiction to alcohol, drugs, sex, stress, or anxiety
- Circumcision, abortion, or organ transplantation
- Consuming large amounts of medication
- Witnessing a tragedy or an abusive situation
- Victim of a motor vehicle accident
- Victim of physical, mental, or sexual abuse
- History of a head injury, loss of consciousness, or near-death experience

BEHAVIORAL
- Feeling "stuck" in your life
- Blocked creativity or sexuality
- Chronic stress, exhaustion or fatigue

- Frequent mood swings
- Constant distractions of the mind
- Sudden onset of road rage
- Profound grief or depression
- Desire to injure self or suicidal thoughts
- Chronic negative thinking

PSYCHIC EXPERIENCE

- People under psychic attack
- Frequently working in the energy fields of others
- Sleep disturbances, night terrors or sleepwalking
- Experimentation with occult phenomena
- Intrusive recurring dreams
- Difficulty disengaging from a relationship
- Feelings of intense anger, fear, or long-standing inertia
- Lack of discipline with a spiritual regimen
- History of psychiatric illness with hospitalization
- People who are "stuck" spiritually

Vulnerabilities to Outside Interferences

The following situations create auric weaknesses that can magnetize negative energies.[1]

1. **Physical**

Drugs or prescription medication	Transplants
Alcohol	Chronic stress or exhaustion
Accident(s)	Difficult birth
Injury	Loss of consciousness
Abortion(s)	Sexual act(s)
Serious Illness	Cemetery or hospital visits

2. **Emotional**

Death of a loved one

Shock treatments

Abusive relationship

Past trauma situation

Profound grief

History of psychiatric illness

Depression

Loneliness

Suicidal thoughts

Challenge or dare

Long-standing anxiety

Fear

Betrayal

Repressed emotions

3. **Mental**

Loss of control

Loss of purpose

Loss of money

Loss of sleep

Loss of business

Loss of motivation

Loss of career

Loss of humor

Loss of home

Loss of belief in self

4. **Spiritual**

Astral travel

Lack of protection

Channeling

Spiritual inertia

Spiritual confusion

Psychic attack

Plea for assistance

Past-life remembrances

Intrusive dreams

Séances

Lack of discernment

Awareness of parallel life

Interdimensional travel

Experimentation with psychic phenomena

Near death experience

5. <u>**Sensory**</u>

Annoying sounds	Witnessing violence
Disturbing words	Upsetting images
Irritating conversations	Disturbing movies
Harassing phone calls	Distressing memories

Do You Need an Archangel Clearing?

Take this short quiz to determine the level of necessity to have an Archangel Clearing. Answer these questions from the perspective of early childhood to the present time, to reflect on your entire life experience. The number of "yes" responses will give you an idea of the necessity to have an Archangel Clearing performed.

YES / NO

_____ Do you have a low energy level?

_____ Do you have mood swings or character shifts?

_____ Do you have "inner chatter" in your mind?

_____ Have you ever experimented with drugs, including alcohol?

_____ Do you exhibit impulsive behavior?

_____ Have you had a sudden onset of anxiety or depression for no reason?

_____ Did you ever have a blow to the head?

_____ Do you experience poor concentration?

_____ Have you ever been in any type of accident?

_____ Did you ever visit a cemetery, hospital, nursing home, or funeral?

Scoring

(# of Yes answers)

> **7+:** You have acquired significant negativity and would benefit from an Archangel Clearing.

> **5:** You have some serious blockages. An Archangel Clearing is highly recommended.

> **3:** You have accumulated negative energy. An Archangel Clearing would remove it.

> **Below 3:** Congratulations! You are a rarity!

Explanations of the Archangel Clearing® Technique

The Archangel Clearing Technique is a systematic method for removing various types of negative energy that you may have accumulated during your lifetime. I've registered the name of this remote process with the US Patent and Trademark Office. For this process to be effective, it must be exactly followed as it is presented in this book. Any shortcuts or deletions of steps may render the process to be incomplete or ineffective.

In my first book, *Spiritual Clearings: Sacred Practices to Release Negative Energy and Harmonize Your Life,* the focus was spiritual empowerment for an individual with the procedure for performing Self-Spiritual Clearings. It did not contain information about the correct process to use for a remote Clearing of another individual as it is more complicated. It is essential to know that all types of Archangel Clearings are done remotely. To proceed, permissions must be obtained from both a person's Higher Self **and** from the Universe. In this manner, the person performing the Archangel Clearings will not absorb the karma of another nor will keep the other person from learning any valuable lessons that they agreed to during this incarnation or from Spiritual contracts.

It is of prime importance for a person to perform a Self-Clearing **before** they can perform one for another individual. Each Archangel Clearing is akin to peeling one layer off an onion, so frequent Archangel Clearings are recommended. The steps for performing a Self-Clearing are listed as the first procedure.

To begin the Archangel Clearing Process, it is essential that you create a quiet sacred place by whatever means you have available. It is important to have a white candle to use during the process, and a votive candle will be adequate. Then make sure that you will not be disturbed by the phone or other interruptions such as children, pets, or distracting noises.

The Archangel Clearing begins by centering yourself and requesting spiritual protection and guidance during the process as the entire process takes about an hour. The next step is to increase your vibratory rate. The increase in vibrations is accomplished by stating the specific prayers and chants listed in this book and will enable you to connect more easily with the heightened energies of the Beings of Light of the Spiritual Clearing Team.

After your vibrations are increased, it is time to call forth the specific Advanced Beings who are assigned by Source to assist with these unique Archangel Clearings on the earth plane. Substituting any of these highly evolved Beings of Light would change the spiritual synergy of the process. Omitting any of these same Beings would be detrimental to the strength of the collective spiritual group. However, if you feel strongly about an Ascended Master or specific prayers, contact and add them after the others that have been listed.

Then with your intention, see, sense, or imagine yourself entering the sacred and protective Chamber of the Divine Council of Universes. This Chamber is a protected spiritual inner space that has been provided for this work. Its existence was received in my meditation. Use all your senses to assist you in mentally placing yourself in this protective space. If you don't have "inner vision," do not be concerned. Just use your intention or imagination to enter the sacred chamber. Then call forth the protection of the various sources available to you. While in this sacred Chamber, you will obtain the two necessary permissions to enable you to perform the Archangel Clearing Technique. The Archangel Clearings of others must be done with unconditional love for the other person, a desire for improved communication and interaction between the two people, and a request to the Higher Self that the work serves the highest good of all concerned. Interference for selfish or manipulative reasons or the possibility of personal gain creates a very undesirable karmic burden.[2]

With the use of a pendulum, you can discover which specific energies are interfering with your free will or the free will of the person receiving the Archangel Clearing. This can be accomplished by scanning the list of Categories as you use your pendulum. A checklist of all categories is provided for your convenience in gathering this information. I recommend that you make several copies of this checklist to have available before you begin. As each Category is confirmed with your pendulum, request that each of the assembled members of the Archangel Clearing Team individually remove it into the Light.

However; if it is too confusing or too stressful to use a pendulum or any of the methods of dowsing discussed in Chapter Six (Dowsing Options), just read aloud each category on the list and command that it be removed. The Spiritual Clearing Team has been removing these negative categories with me for over 28 years and knows the entire process. Consequently, there is no way that you can do this Archangel Clearing Technique incorrectly if you follow the exact steps and read aloud everything that is written in the bold font. After you release each type of negative energy, take a few seconds to reflect, or notice, any changes or visualizations that might accompany each release.

As you proceed down the list of categories, you will see that the last listing is a variety of emotions. As you develop your intuition and psychic gifts, you might notice that you can tell where the feeling is stored. From my experience, each of the listed emotions has a color vibration that represents it. Use the power of your imagination to visualize each of these colors as they are released from the chakras and the aura.

It is not common knowledge, but at the base of our skull is a psychic door. Ideally, it is to remain closed at all times. Each of us has a gatekeeper assigned just to keep this psychic door closed. Unfortunately, this door can be opened if there is an accident, operation, blow to the head, drug or alcohol use, or a sudden physical or psychological shock.[3] Please review the previous lists of _Vulnerabilities to Outside Influences_ for other possibilities. For those who are psychic, there are no worries that your intuitive skills will be diminished by this process as your highest source of intuitive information comes from your heart and your crown chakras.

When any of these circumstances occur, the gatekeeper may no longer be adequate and might even disappear. Then this psychic opening becomes a revolving door for negative energies to come and go. This space can create mood swings, confusion, sudden extreme anger, deep depression, or several other symptoms. It is not unusual for the psychic door to be opened during the birth experience, as that is our first trauma. It can also be opened when falling off a swing or bicycle in childhood. Consequently, it is essential to clear out the psychic debris in this area, obtain a new gatekeeper, and then seal the Psychic door closed.[4]

At this time, the healing portion of the Archangel Clearing process will occur. Move through the remaining steps stating aloud your intention to release cords and any lingering unforgiveness; renounce past life vows, and unblock cash flow lines. It is essential to do all these steps every time you perform a Self-Clearing, as you have accumulated these energies throughout many lifetimes. After all the releases have occurred, it is necessary to address the ego. The ego often feels threatened when you embark on your spiritual journey and needs reassurance that it will not be abandoned. By reassuring the ego and moving it aside, your perception of your reality may significantly change. Since it has helped you to survive for all these years, the ego often appreciates this acknowledgment that is read aloud in the script.

After all the phases of the healing have been addressed, it is time to place the protective force fields around everyone who is experiencing an

Archangel Clearing. Just read <u>each protection command verbally</u>, utilizing imagery or your imagination to strengthen the intention whenever possible.

After the Clearing has been performed, please note that the protective force field must be intentionally placed daily around each person who received an Archangel Clearing, to hold the new energetic space. If the person that is experiencing the Archangel Clearing is not aware that it has happened, then it is your responsibility to provide this daily protection for them. It is imperative that this protection becomes part of your daily spiritual hygiene; and it will be necessary to implement this spiritual protection practice at least twice a day. State the shield statement before going to sleep at night and again as you start your day.

Throughout the day if you feel yourself in any discordant energy, mentally call forth the protection-. Intend that the three concentric Bubbles of Protection surround you. The first is Blue and represents Divine Power. The next bubble layer is Gold, representing Divine Wisdom. The outer bubble is Pink, and that represents Divine Love. You may also wish to place these protective spheres around each of your family members, home, and pets daily. Again, use your intention or imagination to visualize this protective energy force field, or say the following prayer: *"Dear Source of All That Is; please place the blue bubble of Divine Power, the gold bubble of Divine Wisdom, and the pink bubble of Divine Love around me* (or another). *Thank you."*

Now that the Archangel Clearing Technique has been completed, it is essential to acknowledge all the Archangels and Highly Evolved Beings who have assisted you with these releases. Thank each of them individually after the Clearing. Next, hold out your hands, with palms facing downward, to allow Mother Earth to use any excess energy for the stability of the planet. Often you might experience the sensation of a magnetic pull on the palms of your hands as the energy is absorbed into the Earth.

Lastly, disconnect from the Beings of Light that assisted you by eliciting an "OM" as you release any attachments to the outcomes of what have transpired.

Chapter Three
Personal Archangel Clearings

The Archangel Clearing Technique (ACT) is designed to remove negative energies that influence an individual, a property, a business, or an animal. This Archangel Clearing Technique is divided into two areas: personal and property. Each process has its manual. A pendulum and a white candle will be needed for both Clearings.

Personal Clearings

Negative energies impact daily living and your quality of life. ACT Personal Clearings consist of 20 steps and usually take an hour or more to complete.

IT IS IMPORTANT THAT YOU <u>ALWAYS </u>PERFORM A CLEARING FOR YOURSELF BEFORE PERFORMING A CLEARING FOR OTHERS OR ANY PROPERTY!

There is a Universal Law with Spirit, which states that you cannot heal another of any injury if you have not cured it in yourself. Spirit has advised that before you start to Clear or treat another with this process that you perform an Archangel Clearing on yourself—to remove anything from your energy field that may create misalignments for you when executing an Archangel Clearing for another.

Clearing of others must be done with unconditional love for the other person, a desire for improved communication and interaction between the two people, and a request to the Higher Self that the work serves the highest good of all concerned. Interference for selfish or manipulative reasons or the possibility of personal gain creates a very undesirable karmic burden.[5]

Remember, you must always obtain permission from someone else's Higher Self.

Archangel Personal Clearing Technique

Step 1: Creating Sacred Space

Light a white candle (or a votive). Follow all these steps exactly as they are written. There are no shortcuts!

Step 2: Centering and Grounding

State aloud:

Healing Prayer

Dear Source,

I ask to be cleared and cleansed with the White Light, the Green Healing Light, and the Violet Transmuting Light.

For my highest good, I ask that all disharmonious vibrations be removed from this room and home, sealed within their Light, and returned to the Source for purification, never again to re-establish within me or anyone else.

I ask to be used as a channel for healing for

_____ (your name or another's name).

I seek this for _____ (my, his, her)

highest good, within _____ (my,

his, her) own will and within Divine Will.

I ask that this room be surrounded by the White Light, and
that _____ (I, or another) be
surrounded by the White Light and the triple shield of
Universal protection.

At this time, I accept those forces of healing that work
through and with me, allowing only that which serves
Source.[6]

I express gratitude for all my many blessings, above all, the
privilege of serving others.

Amen

State aloud:

I call forth my Soul and ask to be surrounded in the golden sphere
of soul energy. I now link my Soul, with laser lines of Light to:

My Higher Self

My I AM Presence

My Guides and Teachers of 100% Pure Light

All Healing Angels of 100% Pure Light

All Light Workers actively assisting Mother Earth's healing

I now ask to be surrounded with the energy, vibration, and color
of **Divine Power** (blue), **Divine Wisdom** (gold) **& Divine Love** (pink).

Step 3: Establishing Protection

State aloud:

Prayer of Protection

Dear Source: I ask for your Divine protection for me. I ask to be placed in the flask of the golden light of your Grace and that is filled with the bright White Light. I ask that this dwelling be surrounded in the golden dome of your Grace, connecting to the Golden Shield beneath the foundation, and filled with the bright White Light.

State aloud:

Preparation Prayer

I come in love and light to my Higher Self and Guardian Angel of _____ and ask for guidance during this Archangel Clearing process. I ask that only the Truth shall come through. I give my Higher Self permission to access information from wherever it must come. I request that all vibrations and lines of communication now be cloaked.

State aloud:

Pendulum Protection (If a pendulum is used)

I align myself with my I AM Presence.

I link my I AM Presence with SOURCE with lines of Light.

Hold hands in prayer position above head, with pendulum in hands and state aloud:

I place this pendulum in a sealed tube of bright White Light, surrounded by the Violet Transmuting Flame.

I charge this pendulum with the power of SOURCE to give me Truth for the highest and greatest good of everyone involved.

Thank you. Thank you. Thank you.

Now visualize yourself aligning, vertically, with SOURCE. Surround yourself with bright White Light, and Love by stating aloud:

I evoke the Light of SOURCE within. I am a clear and perfect channel for the Universal Mind of SOURCE. Light is my guide.

The Light of SOURCE surrounds me.

The Love of SOURCE enfolds me.

The Power of SOURCE protects me.

The Presence of SOURCE watches over me.

Wherever I AM, SOURCE is!

And all is in Divine order.[7]

State aloud:

Prayer for Guidance

Dear Source, please provide me with the wisdom, clarity, protection, and guidance to do this Archangel Clearing today.

Step 4: Asking Permission

You are now ready to tune into the energy of the person for whom you want to do the Archangel Clearing. Using your pendulum, ask for permission.

State the person's name and address. Clear your mind as well as you can and then create a mental picture of the person. Think of the person until you feel an energy connection or focus on an image or visualization of them. It doesn't matter whether you know what the person looks like or not, as long as you focus on their name and address. Your Higher Self knows who you are focusing on, so ask your Higher Self to tune into the person to be released and ask permission to do the work. You can also tune into the other person's energy yourself by doing the following.

State aloud (with your hand, or a crystal, to your heart):

I want to help you in removing all negativity that is affecting your free will. May I have permission to assist the Angels to release this negative energy?

___Yes ___No

If you obtain another "no" answer, you <u>cannot</u> proceed with the Archangel Clearing Technique. However, you can ask for permission only to close the individual's psychic door. After that, close the session.

Step 5: Raising Vibrations

*State **3 times**, aloud:*

Lord's Prayer

Our Father, who art in heaven, hallowed be thy Name.

Thy kingdom come. Thy will be done, on Earth as it is in heaven.

Give us this day our daily bread.

And forgive us our debts, as we forgive our debtors.

And lead us not into temptation, but deliver us from evil.

For thine is the kingdom and the power, and the glory, forever.

Amen.[8]

State aloud in one breath:

Light, Light, Light! (Repeat **3 times**)

*State **6 times**, aloud:* **Kodoish, Kodoish, Kodoish, Adonai 'Tsebayoth** (Koh-Doh-Eesh, Koh-Doh-Eesh, Koh-Doh-Eesh, Ah-Doh-Nah-Eee Tseh-Bah-Yoth)

(This means: Holy, Holy, Holy, the Lord Hosts.)[9]

*State **9 times**, aloud:* **I AM that I AM**

(This unites the individual with the mind of Source)[10]

*State **9 times**, aloud:* **Om**

(This is the sound of all sounds together.)[11]

*State **9 times**, (aloud)*: **Om Mani Padme Hum** (Om Mah-Nee Pud-May Hoom)

(This means the jewel of consciousness is the lotus of the heart).[12]

Step 6: Invoking the Spiritual Clearing Team

State the following aloud:

Through my divinity of Light, I now call forth:

My Guides & Teachers of 100% pure Light
My I AM Presence
Lord Sananda
Mother Mary
Kwan Yin
Beloved Legions of Light
Master St. Germain
The Great White Brotherhood
Archangel Michael and all his legions to the front of me
Archangel Raphael and all his legions to the right of me
Archangel Uriel and all his legions behind me
Archangel Gabriel and all his legions to the left of me
Archangel Jophiel above me
Archangel Zadkiel below me
Archangel Chamuel in my heart
Angels of the Violet Fire
The Deva of Healing

Step 7: Entering the Sacred Chamber

*With great reverence, imagine entering **The Chamber of the Divine Council of Universes**.*

State aloud:

Please form a circle around me and my home and my car and permeate this circle with Unconditional Love. I ask that my vibrations be raised to enable me to attain the wisdom necessary to do this Archangel Clearing.

Step 8: Asking the Universal Permission

Using your pendulum, ask for permission.

State aloud:

Do I have permission to do this Clearing? ___Yes   ___No

If you receive a "no," ask if this is true. If the "no" answer is validated, ask if the psychic door can be closed at this time. (See Step 11 for "Closing the Psychic Door" instructions.) Then ask the Universe to remove any negativity that can be removed; to heal whatever can be healed for the individual's highest good, and to give their Soul what it needs at this time.

If you receive a "yes," using your pendulum, ask the following question.

State aloud:

Do I have the appropriate resources for assistance?

___Yes   ___No

If you receive a "no" answer, please ask for additional Beings of Light to come forward. Using your pendulum, ask the following question:

Am I protected? ___Yes   ___No

If you receive a "no" answer, please ask for your vibrations to be raised and request that another layer of protection be placed around you.

State aloud:

Please raise my vibrations sufficiently to attain the wisdom and clarity necessary to do this Clearing. Please place me in the Triple Shield of Universal protection, surrounded by Violet Fire.

Step 9: Removing Categories

<u>Please note</u>: Definitions for each category are listed in the glossary of this book.

Call the person who is receiving the Clearing into the Chamber of the Divine Council of Universes. Request that they are accompanied by their Higher Self and Guardian Angel. Ask that these Beings explain the process that will occur, to the person receiving this Archangel Clearing.

State aloud:

Past, present, future throughout all time, all realms, all creations, all universes, and all dimensions; real or imagined; known and unknown, I call forth all negative energy categories that are interfering with my (or another's) **free will on any dimension or any level of existence.**

Using the pendulum, State: **Do I** *(or another)* **have any?** *(Read **each** category aloud).*

Using the pendulum, name each category on the checklist and <u>circle the ones on the list that are present</u>. When finished, release each circled energy separately.

Please Note: For each category that is circled, state the following aloud:

I request the removal of_____.

Then start at the top of the following list and read each category, while dowsing with your pendulum or dowsing technique. If not dowsing, then just read each Category aloud and request that it be removed.

NEGATIVE ENERGY CATEGORIES

1. Connection to Mass Consciousness
2. Energy Implants : In chakras or in aura
3. Bondage
4. Manipulations
5. Programming
6. Energy cords
7. Psychic bonding
8. Interference with thought patterns
9. Vibrational influences
10. Codes
11. Discarnate souls
12. Inner conflicts
13. Members of the dark brotherhood
14. Residents
15. Energy band
16. Fakers
17. Arch demons
18. Satanic energies
19. Curse
20. Inner shadow
21. Overshadow
22. Locks
23. Negative essences
24. Negative thought forms
25. False beliefs
26. Electromagnetic interference

27. Negative high levels
28. Highly evolved dark masters
29. Psychic Shocks to chakras & aura
30. Dark angels
31. Astral influences
32. Prejudices
33. Negative energizer
34. Killer psychic energies
35. Demonic presences
36. Auric weaknesses or holes
37. Force fields
38. Interference with cash flow lines
39. Psychic vampires
40. Telepathic pathways
41. Past life binds
42. Auric webbing
43. Frequency controls
44. Self-inflicted thought forms
45. Fragmented souls
46. Encased life energies
47. Accumulated negative energies
48. Unnamed negative energies
49. Open Psychic door
50. Emotions: anger, grief, worry, fear, confusion, anxiety, depression, guilt, hatred, rage, despair, shame, doubt, jealousy, loneliness, suspicion, distrust, greed, resentment, other

Release of Stuck Emotions

State the following aloud:

I command removal of each of the following emotions (list the circled feelings) **with grace and ease for my** (or another's) **Highest Good.**

The negative emotions, along with the colors of the emotions, are included below. See, feel or imagine each of the corresponding colors being released from the physical body as the feelings are also released. These emotions can be stored anywhere; however, these are the most common sites for each.[13]

Anger – red – liver – 3rd chakra, bladder

Fear – blue-gray – kidney, knees, 1st chakra, psoas, trapezius

Depression – black – heart, elbows, all chakras

Anxiety – reddish orange – adrenals, colon, bladder, 1st chakra

Guilt – blue-gray – skin, solar plexus, heart

Confusion – yellow – gall bladder

Distrust – orange yellow – diaphragm

Loneliness – blue-gray – lungs, 4th chakra

Rage – deep red – liver, colon, heart

Despair – grayish yellow – lungs, shoulders, small intestine

Doubt – light blue-gray – low back

Resentment – orange – bladder

Grief – blue-gray – lungs

Hatred – black – liver, gall bladder

Jealousy – yellow – heart, heart chakra

Remorse – dark gray – colon

Greed – dark red – spleen

Worry – blue-gray – pancreas, ankles

Shame – orange – ovaries or testes

Lack/limitation – gray – lack of love in heart; lack of fulfillment, stomach

State aloud: **I command the removal of anything else that was not mentioned, but needs to be released from me** (or another) **now!**

Step 10: Checking Releases

Using your pendulum ask:

Have all Categories been removed? ___Yes ___No

If not state forcefully:

I now hand this situation over to the appropriate authorities to deal with it, according to the hierarchy and laws of the Universe.

Step 11: Closing Psychic Door

Using your pendulum, ask the following (checking the psychic door). **Remember to close your psychic door, before you close another's.**

State:

Is my (or another's) **psychic door open?** ___Yes ___No

Is there a gatekeeper? ___Yes ___No

If there is no gatekeeper, ask your (or another's) Higher Self and Solar Angel to obtain a new gatekeeper.

State:

I ask for the removal of all habits, patterns, and conditioning of any entities and that they are released from the deep cellular layers of my (or another's) body and from my (or another's) subconscious mind.

I ask that these energies be cut free and reamed out from the psychic door area, now.

I ask that my (or another's) aura and spiritual bodies are swept clear now.

I ask that the Golden Light of Source fill my (or another's) psychic door and that my (or another's) psychic door be sealed now with the bright White Light and the Infinity symbol. (Visualize the Infinity Symbol as the # 8, lying sideways)

Using your pendulum, verify that a gatekeeper is in place.

State:

Gatekeeper, please keep this door shut at all times. Thank you for accepting this responsibility. God bless you.

Step 12: Healing of Ego

Using your pendulum, ask if your (or another's) ego needs healing. If yes, state:

I ask the Healing Angels to come forward and give my, (or another's) ego all that it needs so it may heal <u>on all levels</u>. Please heal any original sin, blemishes or stains on my (or another's) soul.

Step 13: Removing Cords

State aloud:

I command the removal of all:

Cord(s)

Attachment(s)

Psychic bonding(s)

Fondness for ____ (insert name) ____

Memories of ____ (insert name) ____

Hate and anger for ____ (insert name) ____

Vibrations

Frequencies

Energy pathways

I command removal of any connections that would ever have these energies return.

I call upon the Psychic Surgeons to remove any remnants or residue, caused by any cords, attachments or implants and to repair any damage to my (or another's) four lower bodies and my (or another's) aura.

Step 14: Invoking the Law of Forgiveness

State aloud:

I now call upon the Law of Forgiveness to erase the cause, the core, the effect, the record, and the memory of all negativity permanently and completely; past, present, and future throughout all time; all realms, all creations, all universes, and all dimensions; real or imagined, known or unknown.

I invite _____:

1. To release themselves of all judgment of self.
2. To release themselves of all judgment of others.
3. To now claim grace.

I now call upon the Ascended Master St. Germain to direct the Transmuting Violet Flame towards any remaining negativity, transmuting it into pure light and unconditional Love.

Step 15: Renouncing Vows

State aloud:

I now ask for the Source's assistance in calling forth any vows and attachments made intentionally or unintentionally by me (or another) **to all overshadows and groups or organizations that** I (or another) **have ever been a member of in any lifetime.**

I now ask Source to assist me (or another) **in the renouncing and revoking of all vows of:**

Fraternity/sisterhood
Alliance
Allegiance
Celibacy
Chastity
Marriage
Obedience
Poverty
Secrecy
Vengeance
Responsibility
Isolation
Power
Silence
Loyalty
Suffering
Subservience
Contracts/pacts/oaths/agreements

And all other vows or attachments of any nature or needs for vows which are no longer for my (or another's) **highest and greatest good.**

Step 16: Unblocking Cash Flow Lines

State aloud **(personal)***:*

> I command the removal of all blockages to my (or another's) personal cash flow lines and that my (or another's) **cash flow lines be fully opened NOW!**

> I command that my (or another's) **personal cash flow lines** now be flooded with luminous White Light

> I ask that my (or another's) **personal cash flow lines be surrounded by the Triple Shield of Universal Protection and then surrounded by the Violet Fire NOW!**

State aloud **(business)***:*

> I command removal of all blockages to the cash flow lines of *(State business name here)* **and that the cash flow lines be fully opened NOW!**

> I command that the cash flow lines to *(state business name here)* now be flooded with luminous White Light

> I ask that the cash flow lines to *(state business name here)* **be surrounded by the Triple Shield of Universal Protection and then be surrounded by Violet Fire. I ask that this business attract the appropriate paying clients and that this business is now financially successful.**

Step 17: Healing

State aloud:

I call upon the Violet Fire to blaze over and transmute any remaining negativity, remnants, or residue. I ask that White Light be spun into any damaged areas.

Now you will focus on the healing of the chakras by stating aloud:

I ask for an activation of each chakra:

    a. A cleansing
    b. A clearing
    c. A healing
    d. A balancing

Please spin White Light into the front and back of each chakra.

I ask this White Light to remain until it sustains the highest frequency of Light possible for myself (or another)

I ask to anchor the correct color ray to each chakra:[14]

    Red for the Root chakra
    Orange for the Sacral Chakra
    Yellow for the Solar Plexus Chakra
    Green for the Heart chakra
    Blue for the Throat chakra
    Indigo for the Brow Chakra
    Violet for the Crown chakra

I ask that each chakra be set spinning correctly, and opened and brought into full functioning power.

State aloud (additional healing):

I call upon the Cosmic Physician:

To remove debris and patterns from my (or another's) **aura, emotional bodies, mental bodies, and mind compartments.**

To repair any holes or weaknesses in the aura.

To heal any body parts, systems, or conditions.

To continue the healing until it is completed.

I call upon the Angelic Beings to assist me (or another) with any healing that is appropriate at the Soul level.

I call upon the Cosmic Physician to restore the perfect pattern of my (or another's) **body, mind, and spirit.**

Step 18: Establishing Bubbles of Protection

State aloud:

I command that a bubble be placed around me (or another) and that **Blue Light** stream through and fill this entire bubble, forming a grid on the interior of the bubble. I command that **Gold Light** stream through the bubble continuing to create the grid, and I command that **Pink Light** stream through and immerse this entire space now.

I command that all energy that is no longer for the highest good be released and sent to the Light now.

I command that only those energies that are for the highest good be allowed to exist within this bubble from this point forward.

I command that only the Beings of Light may change these commands to bring about an even greater good.[15]

Step 19: Expressing Gratitude

State aloud:

In the name of Light, I give thanks to all the Beings who assisted me with this Archangel Clearing today. I say Thank You and Amen to:

My Guides and teachers of 100% pure Light
My I AM Presence
Lord Sananda
Mother Mary
Kwan Yin
Beloved Legions of Light
Master St. Germain
The Great White Brotherhood
Archangel Michael
Archangel Raphael
Archangel Uriel
Archangel Gabriel
Archangel Jophiel
Archangel Zadkiel
Archangel Chamuel
Angels of the Violet Fire
The Deva of Healing

Step 20: Closing

While holding your hands out with palms faced down, ask Mother Earth to take and utilize any extra energy for the healing of the planet.

Chant the word: **OM (3 times)** through your intention to release all attachments and expectations about the results of the Clearing as you chant this holy sound.

Exit (Self and others) **from the** *Chamber of the Divine Council of Universes.*

Blow out the candle and **ground yourself** with one of the following exercises.

Exercises for Grounding

1. Heaven and Earth

- Get as comfortable as possible while sitting in a chair with your feet firmly on the floor.
- Imagine that you are a mighty tree, i.e., a grandfather oak or redwood. Visualize your roots dividing into two major sections.
- Send these roots down through your feet to the earth and anchor them into the bedrock at the earth's core.
- As you inhale, imagine that you are drawing up vibrant and nurturing earth energy. Give it a color, if you wish.
- Imagine that it is filling up your entire physical body and each chakra to the top of your head.
- As you exhale, allow this energy to mix with the power of the Universe.
- Now imagine a radiating White Light above the top of your head.
- Allow it to cascade into your body, as though your body were a glass vessel.
- Visualize or imagine this White Light moving down from your feet into the core of the earth.
- Repeat this complete cycle three or four times.

2. Cable Grounding

- Get as comfortable as you are able while seated in a chair. Make sure your feet are flat on the floor.

- Imagine that you have a cable attached to each hip and another one attached to your tailbone.

- Visualize all three cables dropping down through the floor into the very core of the earth.

- Allow these cables to now be anchored firmly, with massive hooks, into the bedrock of the earth.

- Now imagine the feeling of a dense forest moving up through these cables into your feet and lower torso,

- Carry this "anchoring thought" with you throughout the day.

3. Alignment Exercise

- Start from a seated position with your feet flat on the ground and take three deep breaths.

- Focus your attention on your first chakra at the base of your spine. Notice that this is the center of gravity within your physical body.

- Now imagine all of your chakras aligned in a vertical column from the top of your head to the base of your spine.

- Once all the chakras are in this position, imagine that they turn into a massive core of Light, attaching you to your I AM Presence.[16]

Accelerated Healing

Immediately after an Archangel Clearing, people can experience different phenomena. The most common is a feeling of inner calmness and the sense that a burden has been lifted. Frequently there is increased energy and vibrancy to life. Often people think and sleep better. Mood swings are also common as suppressed and repressed emotions surface. Sometimes a person will start crying uncontrollably for no apparent reason. Others may experience headaches, nausea, fatigue, or flu-like symptoms. These physical symptoms usually last about 48 hours and then will convert to a feeling of peace, harmony, freedom, and well-being. Typically, the symptoms occur within 3-7 days after the Archangel Clearing date.

In general, deep healing may take from several days to several weeks or more to integrate fully. Most often, this is followed by greater spiritual awareness and transformation on the physical, emotional, mental, and spiritual levels. Due to the intensity of the Archangel Clearing process, healing is accelerated at the cellular level of the body. Chakras are cleansed, healed, and balanced, and negative emotions are released from the body and auric field. There may be some physical discomfort during this time. The key to remember is these symptoms are all positive signs that the body is healthy enough to heal itself and re-establish equilibrium. As the layers of energy begin transforming and releasing on the physical, emotional, mental, and spiritual levels, an overall balancing occurs. Once this process is allowed to follow its natural course, health is regained, and a tremendous feeling of wholeness, strength, and inner harmony ensues. To facilitate the release of stuck or stagnant emotions, please use the following form of spiritual self-empowerment.

Emotional Release

To facilitate the release of stuck or stagnant emotions, please use the following process for spiritual self-empowerment.

Identify the dominant emotion that you are experiencing. Be precise. Do not use general terms like 'feeling bad.' Once the emotional state is identified, state the following: *"I do not accept this* (state the emotion)! *I send it back to the sender, one thousand-fold with divine love!"* State this phrase <u>three</u> times with emphasis.

If the emotion does not disappear after the three decrees, then it is probably your own emotion either coming up to be released or to be healed. If so, state the following: *Thank you* (state the feeling) *for all the lessons you have taught me. I will preserve the learning. You are no longer needed. I release you now and command you to leave!*

Imagine this release like black puffs of smoke exiting from the top of your head as the emotion leaves your body and awareness.

Now cleanse your body by imagining a waterfall of shimmering White Light above your head that is filling your entire body with Light. It is as though your body is a glass vessel. Imagine any other remnants or residue of the emotion being washed out through your hands and feet into the Universe to be re-qualified.

Chapter Four
Home and Business Archangel Clearings

Archangel Clearings for dwellings and property are designed to release negative energies that influence a home, a property, a business, an object, or an animal. A pendulum and a white candle will also be needed for this Clearing.

Negative energies impact not only your daily living and your quality of life, but also your home, business, property, and pets. ACT Home and Business Clearings usually take an hour. It is designed to be read aloud as a script. To be the most effective, follow the sequence written and do not omit any of the steps.

Several situations may require a Home and Business Clearing:

- A building feels haunted.
- It is located next to a cemetery or hospital.
- It is an historical home or building.
- Previously a rental property.
- Death or abuse occurred.
- Property is being disputed (divorce, etc.).
- It is furnished with used furniture.
- Pet died shortly after moving in.
- Many parties or large gatherings.

- Onset of unusual fear or anger after moving in.
- It is decorated with antiques or heirlooms.
- Rooms or areas feel creepy.
- Usage of rented convalescent equipment.
- Onset of being tired or depressed after moving in.
- Vacant for an extended period.
- Was a former 'crack' house or meth lab
- Behavioral change in animals or pets.
- It contains artifacts from foreign countries.

Situations that May Require a Home and Property Archangel Clearing

Frequently, homes that have been on the market for a considerable amount of time are filled with disharmonious energies and thought forms. This situation is especially true of the discordant energies found in homes that are sold due to divorce or foreclosure. Negative energy can be left by former tenants, or it can be brought to a place by workers or visitors. Soon after you purchase a new home, and before you move in, is the best time to do a house and property Clearing. Other situations are as follows:

- Houses that haven't sold for any apparent reason
- Avoiding certain rooms or areas in your home
- Dwellings that contain antiques
- Feeling exhausted when at home, but nowhere else
- Rental properties
- Poor concentration only when at home
- Owners who were reluctant to sell the house due to partnership dissolution.
- Location is near a cemetery, funeral parlor or hospital
- Discomfort with the home's atmosphere or vibrations
- A death or tragedy occurred at the site

- Difficulty sleeping or nightmares since moving to a new home
- Previous occupants had a severe lingering illness
- Behavior changes or sickness in your pets since moving to a new place
- Homes with books, paintings, and artifacts from other countries
- Former occupants were addicted to alcohol or drugs
- Disputes with neighbors since moving in
- Houses that feel "haunted."
- Experiencing waves of fear when home alone

Situations that May Require a Business Archangel Clearing

Negative energy can also be found in business settings where a group of individuals interacts with different goals, values, and belief systems, whether they are employees, management, or customers. Other situations are as follows:

Changes in Business Structure

- Recent merger, acquisition or reorganization
- Reduction in cash flow lines of business
- Business owner is going through a divorce
- Programs or product lines are inefficient and ineffective
- Real estate obtained through inheritance
- Business is for sale or was recently moved to a different site
- Property or real estate with strong family ties

Employee Attitudes and Life Changes

- High employee turnover
- Recent layoffs or terminations
- Feeling energetically uncomfortable in parts of the building
- Feeling "drained" when at the work site
- Lack of creativity or low morale
- Employees frequent bars or abuse drugs
- Disgruntled or cynical employees or dissension among employees
- Carelessness resulting in an undesirable safety record

Customer Patterns

- High consumer traffic pattern
- Presence of emotional outbursts from customers
- Areas where accidents have occurred
- Dwellings at the site of previous altercations or abuse
- Amusement parks or historical attractions
- Entrances to buildings where energy is stagnant
- Tourist attractions where negative energies accumulate

Archangel Home and Business Clearing Technique

REMEMBER: IT IS IMPORTANT THAT YOU ALWAYS PERFORM AN ARCHANGEL CLEARING FOR YOURSELF BEFORE CLEARING OTHERS OR PROPERTY!

There is a Universal Law with Spirit, which states that you cannot heal another of any injury if you have not healed it in yourself. Spirit has advised that before you start to Clear or treat another with this process that you perform an Archangel Clearing on yourself, to remove anything from your energy that may create misalignments for you when executing an Archangel Clearing for another.

Step 1: Creating Sacred Space

Find a quiet space where you will not be interrupted. Light a white candle. Follow these steps exactly as they are written and do not take any shortcuts.

Step 2: Centering and Grounding

Recite aloud:

Healing Prayer

Dear Source of All That Is,

I ask to be cleared and cleansed with the White Light, the Green Healing Light, and the Violet Transmuting Light.

For my highest good, I ask that all disharmonious vibrations be removed from this room and home, sealed within their Light, and returned to the Source for purification; never again to re-establish within me or anyone else.

I ask to be used as a channel for healing for

_____ (your name or another's name or animal). **I seek this for** _____ (my, his, her, animal) **highest good, within**

_____ (my, his, her, animal) **own will and within Divine Will.**

I ask that this room be surrounded by the White Light, and that _____ (I, another, or animal) be surrounded by the White Light and the triple shield of Universal protection.

At this time, I accept those forces of healing that work through and with me, allowing only that which serves Source.

I express gratitude for all my many blessings, above all, the privilege of serving others.[17]

Amen

State the following aloud:

I call forth my Soul and ask to be surrounded in the golden sphere of soul energy. I now link my Soul, with laser lines of Light to:

My Higher Self

My I AM Presence

My Guides and Teachers of 100% Pure Light

All Healing Angels of 100% Pure Light

All Light Workers actively assisting Mother Earth's healing

I now ask to be surrounded with the energy, vibration, and color of **Divine Power** (blue), **Divine Wisdom** (gold) & **Divine Love** (pink).

Step 3: Establishing Protection

State aloud:

Prayer of Protection

Dear Source: I ask for your Divine protection for me. I ask to be placed in the flask of the golden light of your Grace and that it be filled with the bright White Light. I ask that this dwelling be surrounded in the golden dome of your Grace, connecting to the Golden Shield beneath the foundation, and filled with the bright White Light.

State aloud:

Preparation Prayer

I come in love and light to my Higher Self, and I AM Presence and ask for guidance during this Archangel Clearing process. I ask that only the Truth shall come through. I give my Higher Self permission to access information from wherever it must come. I request that all vibrations and lines of communication now be cloaked.

State aloud:

Pendulum Protection (If a pendulum is used)

I align myself with my I AM Presence.

I link my I AM Presence with SOURCE with lines of light.

Hold hands in prayer position above head, with pendulum in hands and state aloud:

I place this pendulum in a sealed tube of bright White Light, surrounded by the Violet Transmuting Flame.

I charge this pendulum with the power of SOURCE to give me Truth for the highest and greatest good of everyone involved.

Thank you. Thank you. Thank you.

Now visualize yourself aligning, vertically, with SOURCE. Surround yourself with bright White Light, and Love by stating aloud:

I evoke the Light of SOURCE within. I am a clear and perfect channel for the Universal Mind of SOURCE. Light is my guide.

The Light of SOURCE surrounds me.

The Love of SOURCE enfolds me.

The Power of SOURCE protects me.

The Presence of SOURCE watches over me.

Wherever I AM, SOURCE is!

And all is in Divine order.[18]

State aloud:

Prayer for Guidance

Dear Source, please provide me with the wisdom, clarity, protection, and guidance to do this Archangel Clearing today.

Step 4: Raising Vibrations

*State **3 times**, aloud:*

Lord's Prayer

Our Father, who art in heaven, hallowed be thy Name.

Thy kingdom come. Thy will be done, on Earth as it is in heaven.

Give us this day our daily bread.

And forgive us our debts, as we forgive our debtors.

And lead us not into temptation, but deliver us from evil.

For thine is the kingdom and the power, and the glory, forever and ever.

Amen.[19]

State aloud in one breath:

Light, Light, Light! (Repeat **3 times**)

*State **6 times**, aloud:* **Kodoish, Kodoish, Kodoish, Adonai 'Tsebayot** (Koh-Doh-Eesh, Koh-Doh-Eesh, Koh-Doh-Eesh, Ah-Doh-Nah-Eee Tseh-Bah-Yoth)

(This means: Holy, Holy, Holy is the Lord God of Hosts.)[20]

*State **6 times**, aloud:* **I AM that I AM**

(This unites the individual with the mind of Source)[21]

*State **9 times**, aloud*: **Om**

(This is the sound of all sounds together.)[22]

*State **9 times**, aloud*: **Om Mani Padme Hum** (Om Mah-Nee Pud-May Hoom)

(This means the jewel of consciousness is the lotus of the heart).[23]

Step 5: **Invoking the Spiritual Clearing Team**

State the following aloud:

Through my divinity of Light, I now call forth:

My Guides & Teachers of 100% pure Light
My I AM Presence
Beloved Legions of Light
Master St. Germain
The Great White Brotherhood
Pan and the Nature Spirits
Archangel Michael and all his legions to the front of me
Archangel Raphael and all his legions to the right of me
Archangel Uriel and all his legions behind me
Archangel Gabriel and all his legions to the left of me
Archangel Jophiel
Archangel Zadkiel
Archangel Chamuel
Angels of the Violet Fire
Deva of the Earth Kingdom
Deva of (physical address or animal)
Ancestors and Guardians of (physical address)
St. Francis of Assisi (for animals only)

Step 6: Setting Intentions

State aloud:

My intention to bring balance, peace, and harmony to this property (or animal) **and to work in cooperation with the Beings of 100% pure Light, the Archangels, the Spiritual Clearing Team, the Devic Kingdom, the Nature Spirits, Mother Earth and the other energies assisting me today for the highest and greatest good of all.**

Step 7: Asking for Permission

Using your pendulum, first, ask the Universe if you can perform the desired Clearing. Next, mentally tune into the Deva of the property or animal. Using your pendulum, ask the Deva also for permission.

State aloud: **Do I have permission to do this Clearing?** ___Yes ___No

If you receive a "no" answer, please thank all the Spiritual Clearing Team. Release them with gratitude and love, as the Archangel Clearing cannot be done without the Deva's permission. If you receive a "yes," from both the Deva and the Universe, continue with this process.

If you are not using a pendulum, choose one of the device-less dowsing options from the following chapter.

Step 8: Encircling the Clearing Area

State aloud:

I ask that _____ (physical address of property) **be encircled with White Light and permeate this circle, and everything in it, with unconditional love and the**

highest level of cleansing energy. **Please increase it as needed and appropriate throughout the Clearing process. Please enlarge this circle to be greater than the property itself.**

Step 9: Entering the Clearing Chamber

Imagine entering the ***Chamber of the Divine Council of Universes.***

State aloud:

> **Please form a circle around me and my home and my car and permeate this circle with unconditional love. Please place me in the Protective Pillar of Light. Then place me in the Triple Shield of Universal Protection, surrounded by the Violet Fire.**

Step 10: Removing Categories

State aloud:

> **On behalf of** _____ (physical address of property or animal), **I call forth all categories that are interfering with this property** (or animal).

Using the pendulum, state aloud:

> **Does this property** (or animal) **have any?**

Using the pendulum, or another dowsing method, name each category on the checklist and <u>circle the ones that are present on the list</u>. When finished, release each circled energy separately.

Please Note: For each individual category that is circled, state the following aloud:

I command the removal of_____.

I ask the Universe to dissipate, dissolve, and return each of these negative energies to their source on all levels and dimensions across all time and space.

Negative Energy Categories

Demonic Presences

Discarnate Beings

Force fields

Arch demons

Negative thought forms

Negative essences

False Beliefs

Angel of Death

Highly evolved dark masters

Astral influences

Vibrational influences

Telepathic pathways

Satanic energies

Energy cords

Psychic bonding

Accumulated negative energies

Killer psychic energies

Electromagnetic interference

Fragmented souls

Emotions: anger, rage, fear, depression, anxiety, confusion, loneliness, apathy, remorse, greed, divorce energy

Other Negative influence of any type

Step 11: Unblocking the Cash Flow Lines

Please note: This step pertains only to a business or to a real estate sale. (Otherwise, this step can be omitted.)

State aloud:

> **I command removal of all blockages to the cash flow line of**
> _____ (business name or physical address
> of real estate) **and that the cash flow lines are completely
> opened.**
>
> **I command the cash flow lines to**
> _____ (business name or physi-
> cal address of real estate) **now be flooded with bright White
> Light.**
>
> **I ask that the cash flow lines to**
> _____ (business name or physi-
> cal address of real estate) **be surrounded by the Triple Shield
> of Universal Protection and then surrounded by the Violet
> Fire. I ask that this** _____
> (business name or physical address of real estate) **attract the
> appropriate paying client(s) and that this**
> _____ (business name or physi-
> cal address of real estate) **is now financially successful. I ask
> that prosperity flow for the owner's highest good NOW!**

Step 12: Blessing of Location (or animal)

Imagine, or visualize the pink mist of Unconditional Love filling each room (or surrounding the animal).

State aloud:

> **I ask the Archangels to radiate love and blessings into** _____ (physical address of property) **and the environment** (or animal).

Please Note: The following request is optional and may be omitted. **Please bless this dwelling and fill it with the presence of Life, Light, Truth, Health, Prosperity, Peace, and Harmony.**

Step 13: Positioning of Deva

State aloud:

> **I now surround the Deva with the protective concentric circles of Divine Power** (blue), **Divine Wisdom** (gold) **and Divine Love** (pink). **I ask that the Deva be placed over** _____ (business name or physical address of real estate or animal) **and that she stream love down to cover the entire area.**
>
> **I give to you, Deva, a heart and a blue cross to stay anchored in the energy of Love.**

Visualize the positioning of the Deva over the property (or animal). See her holding the blue cross and a Heart. See pink rays of love streaming over the property.

State aloud:

> **Thank you, Deva, for holding this space of Love. God Bless You.**

Step 14: Expressing Gratitude

State aloud:

In the name of Light, I give thanks to all the Beings who assisted me with this Archangel Clearing today. I say Thank You and Amen to:

My Guides, teachers of 100% pure Light
My I AM Presence
Archangel Chamuel
Master St. Germain
Angels of the Violet Fire
The Great White Brotherhood
Pan and the Nature Spirits
Beloved Legions of Light
Archangel Michael and all his legions
Archangel Raphael and all his legions
Archangel Uriel and all his legions
Archangel Gabriel and all his legions
Archangel Jophiel
Archangel Zadkiel
Deva of the Earth Kingdom
Deva of _____ (city of property)
Deva of _____ (physical address)
Ancestors and Guardians of _____ (physical address)
St. Francis of Assisi (for animals only)

While holding your hands out with palms faced down, ask Mother Earth to take and utilize any extra energy from this Archangel Clearing for the healing of the planet.

*State aloud **three times:***

OM or AUM

Blow out the candle, then center and ground yourself with the Exercises for Grounding in the next section.

Exercises for Grounding

Heaven and Earth

- Get as comfortable as possible while sitting in a chair with your feet firmly on the floor.
- Imagine that you are a mighty tree, i.e., a grandfather oak or redwood. Visualize your roots dividing into two major sections.
- Send these roots down through your feet to the earth and anchor them into the bedrock at the earth's core.
- As you inhale, imagine that you are drawing up vibrant and nurturing earth energy. Give it a color, if you wish.
- Imagine that it is filling up your entire physical body and each chakra to the top of your head.
- As you exhale, allow this energy to mix with the power of the Universe.
- Now imagine a radiating White Light above the top of your head.
- Allow it to cascade into your body, as though your body were a glass vessel.
- Visualize, or imagine, this White Light moving down from your feet into the core of the earth.
- Repeat this complete cycle three or four times.

Cable Grounding

- Get as comfortable as you are able while seated in a chair. Make sure your feet are flat on the floor.

- Imagine that you have a cable attached to each hip and another one attached to your tailbone.
- Visualize all three cables dropping down through the floor into the very core of the earth.
- Allow these cables to now be anchored firmly, with massive hooks, into the bedrock of the earth.
- Now imagine the feeling of a dense forest moving up through these cables into your feet and lower torso,
- Carry this "anchoring thought" with you throughout the day.

Alignment Exercise

- Start from a seated position with your feet flat on the ground and take three deep breaths.
- Focus your attention on your first chakra at the base of your spine. Notice that this is the center of gravity within your physical body.
- Now imagine all of your chakras aligned in a vertical column from the top of your head to the base of your spine.
- Once all the chakras are in this position, imagine that they turn into a massive core of Light, attaching you to your I AM Presence.[24]

Chapter Five
Animal Archangel Clearing

It is my understanding that the Animal Kingdom has made a pact with humankind to absorb emotional, mental, and spiritual negativity from the environment. Consequently, house pets work diligently to balance our energy fields by absorbing our negativity. Since pets are living in the human world, they can pick up and experience any challenges we have in our homes. If there is stress in the house, then the animals will feel that stress. They tune into every mood because of their loyalty and service to humanity.

As a result, they are also affected by negative energy on land and in homes. At the same time, it is believed that animals are here to be our examples of unconditional love. Just as humans, animals are exposed to environmental toxins and pollution. They can develop energetic imbalances that can manifest into disease and behavior issues. Often, there is a similarity between a pet's health and the owner's health.

Animals are more receptive than people to the remote Archangel Clearings because they do not have any fixed belief system to block the flow of energy. The Animal Kingdom is naturally far more connected to the earth than humans. After receiving an Archangel Clearing, the outcomes for animals (cats, dogs, horses, birds, and others) are described below:

- Restlessness and stress are alleviated.
- Pets seem happier and more content.

- Scared and high-strung animals are calmer
- Depression and grief are lifted.
- Separation anxiety is reduced.
- Terminally ill pets make their transition easier.
- Some behavioral problems disappear.
- Animals seem more affectionate.

Does Your Pet Need a Clearing?

Please take this short quiz to discern if your farm animal/pet/animal companion would benefit from remote Archangel Clearing.

Point Value for each YES	QUESTION
10	1. Did your pet recently undergo a medical procedure?
10	2. Has there been a sudden onset of destructive behavior?
5	3. Has there been a loss of appetite or interest in usual activities?
10	4. Has your pet been mistreated or traumatized?
5	5. Has there been a recent change in the family routine?
15	6. Is your pet a rescued animal?
10	7. Are there symptoms unexplained by your vet?
5	8. Has another pet died recently?
5	9. Does your pet fear objects (frequent with horses)?
10	10. Is your pet nervous or high strung?

Points	SCORING
50-80 points	Your animal companion has acquired significant levels of negativity and would benefit from an Archangel Clearing.
30-49 points	Your pet has some negative energies and serious energetic imbalances. A remote Archangel Clearing would be highly recommended.
16-29 points	Your pet has accumulated negative energy that needs to be released before behavioral issues ensue. An Archangel Clearing could resolve this situation.
Below 15 points	Your animal must have recently experienced some energy healing by a practitioner.

Archangel Animal Clearing Technique

As stated in the previous chapter, Archangel Clearings for dwellings and property are designed to release negative energies that influence a home, a property, a business, an object, or an animal. When planning a remote Archangel Clearing for an animal, or an inanimate object, such as jewelry, clothing, furniture, toys, or a vehicle, use the same list of Negative Energy Categories that are used in the preceding chapter for ACT Home and Business Clearings. Then proceed to use the appropriate words that will pertain to what you are Clearing. To be the most effective, continue in the sequence as written and do not omit any of the steps. The only addition is to the Spiritual Clearing Team as you will call forth St. Francis of Assisi to minister any healing to the animal instead of the Cosmic Physician.[25] A pendulum and a white candle will also be needed for this Archangel Clearing. If this seems too confusing, rest assured, that the Archangel Clearing Technique cannot be done improperly since the Spiritual Clearing Team has been assisting me with this process for nearly thirty years. The Spiritual Clearing Team has it down and in some cases might be ahead of you in the Archangel Clearing process.

Chapter Six
Dowsing Options

To perform a remote Archangel Clearing for another, you must ask and receive two different permissions: one is from the other person's Higher Self, and the second is from the Universe. Permission will only be granted if the Archangel Clearing is in Divine Order, performed with love, and for the Highest Good. While it is beyond the scope of this book to teach the skill of dowsing or kinesiology, I have briefly listed a few options that the reader may wish to research on his or her own.

Dowsing was initially used as the practice of seeking water with the aid of a forked stick or a similar device. Today, dowsing also applies to the manner of finding information about all kinds of things, not just physical objects or places. Using a pendulum is also considered dowsing.[26] The best way to develop the skill of dowsing is to do it frequently. One of the problems many dowsers have is that they often lack confidence in their dowsing accuracy. As dowsing becomes more popular, there are more people offering courses that will show you techniques and applications that can guarantee the reliability of your dowsing. Also, some books have specific charts for the student to use for skill development. The following information is a brief overview of some of the methods that are available for the reader to explore to obtain information and permissions when performing remote Archangel Clearings.

The main reason it has taken me ten years to write this book is due to the complexity and karmic potential of providing Archangel Clearings for others. Before the creation of this book, the techniques for performing Archangel Clearings for others was only presented through intensive weekend workshops. However, much has changed in our world during the past several years and I believe it is vital for spiritually-evolved individuals to have some useful tools to help family members and friends move out of the grips of negativity and stagnation.

When someone desires to perform an Archangel Clearing for themselves, they need to proceed through the process as previously stated. While it is ideal to obtain verbal permission from another before a Spiritual Clearing is performed, there frequently are situations when a verbal permission might not be obtained. Some of these situations are parents desiring to preform a Spiritual Clearing for a child, or an individual who is very ill, or someone who might not believe in the Angelic World. In such cases when an individual does not have verbal permission to continue with an Archangel Clearing for another; **two** additional permissions are required.

To obtain permission for a remote Clearing for someone that does not directly request one, a dowsing technique is mandatory to communicate with the Universe and gain consent. The dowsing tool I have always used is the pendulum, which requires a certain amount of skill development if you have never used one before for guidance.

Pendulum Basics

We all can access our intuition and psychic gifts by using a pendulum. Learning to use a pendulum is like any other skill. It requires time, determination, and persistent practice. Every object, animate or inanimate, gives off energetic radiations and our expanded awareness can measure these energies.[27] Thus, it is necessary to approach the pendulum with enthusiasm, optimism, and confidence that you can use it.

A pendulum can be made of gold, silver, brass, copper, bronze, or wood. I have always used those made of brass. The best shape to purchase is the type that tapers to a point and is not heavy. The pendulum can move in three different ways: with a circular movement (clockwise or counter-clockwise), elliptical movement, or in a straight line (horizontal or vertical).[28]

Start by holding the chain of your pendulum between your index finger and your thumb. Most people use their dominant hand. I prefer to drape the pendulum chain over my index finger and for balance, I rest my elbow on the arm of the chair or couch as an anchor, so my wrist does not become fatigued.

Clear your mind and "go neutral," as though your mind was a whiteboard that you just erased. To do this, you can tap your thymus on the upper part of the chest before beginning and then wipe your forehead to clear away all extraneous thoughts. Align yourself with your I AM Presence and ask for all information to be directed through the Heart Chakra. Allow this to be your monitoring tool. You will find, as this takes place, that you will be able to feel a shift in your Heart Chakra when the pendulum changes direction. This is one of the ways to know if it is your Will or Ego directing the pendulum, or if it is Source energy doing so.

If you find that you are not feeling a shift in the energy of your Heart in some manner, then the energy is used to move the pendulum is probably coming from your Ego or Mind. If you are affecting the pendulum with your energy, ask to have all fear, all doubt, and all ego be put to the side for the Divine Will of Source and your Will to become in direct alignment as One. This will be helpful to you; however, your best monitoring tool is your heart. If you are feeling your heart shift, this is an energy link from Source, and the information is accurate. If you choose not to become proficient with this Heart-Centered technique, you can still become successful using the pendulum for dowsing answers while performing Archangel Clearings in the sacred chamber.

To start, ask the pendulum to show you what is a "yes" and what is a "no" answer. In the beginning, these movements might be different each time it is used, so write the actions down before actually starting the Archangel Clearing. For most people, "yes" is clock-wise, and "no" is counter-clockwise. "Yes" could also be vertical and "no" horizontal.

If the pendulum swings back and forth instead of counter-clockwise or diagonally (once you establish your "yes" and "no" responses), that means "maybe," so re-phrase the question. Having found which movement is your own 'yes' and 'no' answer, now practice using the dowsing as a technique. In dowsing for beginners, once you establish the "yes" and "no" responses of your pendulum, one of the most important things to test are food and supplements. Hold your pendulum over the food or supplement and ask; "Is this for my highest good?" or "Is this good for my body?" Then practice with any other questions that you wish to ask to build up your dowsing skills.

Any thoughts about possible answers, personal desires, or feelings about the outcome will influence the accuracy of your work. Keeping yourself in a neutral state of detachment to the result is one of the keys to your future success. It is important to start with simple questions about situations or conditions in which you are unemotionally detached from the outcome. Your answers are going to be only as good as the phrasing of your questions, primarily those that are simple and require a 'yes' or 'no' answer. By simple, I am referring to questions that only have one answer, not two questions in one sentence, each requiring its answer. Remember, as with any skill that you have learned; it requires practice, patience and persistence.[29]

Kinesiology

There are many methods of dowsing without using a device, (like a rod) or a tool (like a pendulum). Instead, you will receive neuromuscular signals using your body to answer your questions. Kinesiology, a fancy name for the modality of muscle testing, is one of them. Anyone can use this tool because it uses your electrical system and your muscles. Most position the fingers to receive neuromuscular signals that are interpreted as yes or no answers to simple questions. As with any dowsing method, the response to know for a yes and no answer must be determined before the questions are asked. In virtually all device-less methods, a strong response indicates a 'yes' and a weak response indicates a 'no' answer.[30]

Perhaps you've been the recipient of muscle testing when you've been seen by a chiropractor or another holistic practitioner, who asked you to extend your arm, then asked a question and applied pressure to that arm. If the answer was true, then the extended arm stayed strong. However, if the answer was false, the arm became weak and dropped.

When using any of the following device-less techniques for dowsing answers, it is imperative that you create a method of verifying the validity of your responses to the questions you ask. The easiest method of verification is to state your name, i.e. "My name is _____". Using whichever method you feel proficient with, check for a positive response. Next, state your name as someone else's name, i.e. "My name is _____". Check to verify that the answer is negative since that is not your name.

Other tests for verification of true answers are by stating any truths or untruths that you are already aware of and confirm your positive and negative response.

Since this just a brief overview of some of the methods to utilize muscle testing, I am encouraging the reader to perform his or her own research to develop skill-building techniques.

Finger-Thumb Kinesiology

This is probably the most common way of muscle testing/dowsing that just uses your hand and fingers. It can be done virtually anywhere. The primary importance is that there is a consistent and reliable difference between your 'yes' and 'no' answers. With this method of dowsing, you rub your index finger and thumb together. It only works on dry skin. After you ask a question, the 'yes' answer will feel sticky on your fingers while rubbing them together while a 'no' response will have a rough sensation.[31]

Two Ring Kinesiology

With this method, you make two separate circles with your thumbs and index fingers. First, create a circle by touching the tip of your index finger to the tip of your thumb on your non-dominant hand. Then loop your other thumb in the middle of the first circle and join it together by touching it to your remaining index finger. Now both rings are interlocked like a chain link. Now try to pull the dominant hand circle out through the weakest part of the ring on your non-dominant hand. If the answer to the question is correct, the rings will hold steady and not break apart when gently pulled. However, if the answer to the question asked is false, the links will be weak and pull apart.[32]

Circuit Fingers Kinesiology

This method also uses your fingers, only this time you connect the tip of your left thumb with the tip of your left little (pinkie) finger. Circuit fingers can touch the tip to tip or finger pad to finger pad. Both might feel a bit uncomfortable until you get used to the position. With your left thumb and little finger touching, place the thumb and index finger of your other hand inside this circle you have created. These are your circuit fingers. If the answer to your question is positive, you will be unable to pull apart the circuit fingers easily. Instead, if the answer is negative, the circuit fingers will weaken and separate.[33]

The Snap Kinesiology

With this single-handed muscle-testing technique, press the thumb and a finger of one hand together as if you are about to snap your fingers. Use a firm but not painful pressure and feel the strength between the finger and thumb. Experiment to discern how much weight you need to exert to create a snap for a "no" answer. Once you are clear on the difference between your positive and negative responses, you can begin to use the snap for dowsing answers.[34]

Finger over Finger Kinesiology

Using this method, you place your middle finger over your index finger on the same hand. The index finger is straight with the middle finger bending to touch it. The finger on top will be doing the pushing down, and the finger on the bottom will be resisting the push. If the index finger stays straight it is a "yes" and if the index finger bends downward, then it is a "no". Play with the pressure to discern how much you need to exert for your "yes" and then, your "no" answers.[35]

Okay Sign Kinesiology

Use the index finger of your dominant hand to test the strength of an okay sign formed with the finger and thumb of your non-dominant hand. Insert the index finger of your dominant hand into the okay sign and then try to break the sign open as you determine a positive and then a negative answer. If the okay sign does not collapse, then the answer is "yes." If it does collapse, then the answer is "no."[36]

Ring Finger Kinesiology

With your hand in a vertical position, relax your ring finger, so it is now extended and perpendicular to your hand. Then with the index finger of your opposite hand, test the strength of the ring finger as you ask your questions. If your ring finger stays locked, the answer is "yes." If it bends down, then the answer is "no".[37]

Blink Kinesiology

This technique is also effortless, quick, and does not depend on any tool or even your hands. To use this method, first, look at a blank wall and then take a deep breath. As you do so, relax and soften your eyes. Consciously hold your eyes open. Ask your question, and if you blink against your will the answer is "yes." No blink is a "no" answer. Another variation is one blink for a positive response, two blinks for a negative response.[38]

Intuitive Techniques

Intuitive excellence is based on the first impression you get, so stay with your first impression. Often when people start to get intuitive flashes, they tend to dismiss them and think it is just their mind playing tricks on them. They allow doubt and logic to argue with that intuitive insight. To develop your intuitive excellence, always assume that what you are getting is accurate. Then have enough love for yourself to trust your first intuitive impression, and know that what you are receiving is a correct interpretation from your Higher Self. If you are creative, you might want to make a "spinner" such as those found in children's games. Then make one side a 'yes' and the other side a 'no.' Ask your simple question and then flick the spinner for your answer.

Traffic Light Dowsing

To understand the principle of traffic light dowsing, think of traffic lights —red and green. Using this analogy, your Higher Self can visually show your intuitive self the right response for the question you are asking by giving you a 'yes' (green) or 'no' (red) in reply to your question.

You can use this method of intuitive dowsing for many things, such as choosing the best food for your optimum health. For example, if you are buying produce in a grocery store, intuitively ask your Higher Self for a traffic light response. You might be surprised to find out that the fruit that looks the best to you gives you a red 'no' answer. This answer could mean that they have sprayed with pesticides or other chemicals. If you receive an amber light, that might be an indication that the produce has been stored too long in one place or has lower nutrients or vibration.

You can also use this traffic light dowsing for any specific decision such as the best time to accomplish a task or if you should make a purchase. If you use this system in your daily life, you will enhance your confidence as you will be continuously linked to your Higher Self.

Another version of this method of dowsing is to draw a large circle on a piece of paper and draw a vertical line down the middle of it. Then color one half of the circle green for 'go' or 'yes' and color the other half red for 'stop' or 'no.' Next, ask a question with a yes or no answer. Immediately look at the circle and notice which of the two colors appears to vibrate or even looks 3-D. That will be your 'Yes' answer. A variation is to place your left hand separately over each color of the circle and notice which color causes a sensation in your hand. That will be your 'yes' answer.

Heart-Focus Dowsing

Still another method to follow your intuition, and the one I prefer is by listening to the still, small voice in your heart. When beginning, it is important to clear your heart with prayer, affirmations, or visualization before tuning into it as a means for making intuitive decisions. Elizabeth Clare Prophet's book, *Alchemy of the Heart,* provides healing affirmations to heal any painful past experiences.[39] Other techniques for healing your heart can be found on the internet.

Once your heart is healed, focus on your heart and breathe in and out through it several times as though your heart had a mouth. Then tune in to this center of Source's love within you and notice a sense of peace. Next, ask for your 'yes' and 'no' responses. Trust the very first answer that you obtain.

It is possible that all these techniques may come easily to you. I suggest hat you find the one that is the easiest and most reliable technique for you. Then practice on a regular basis, asking YES or NO questions for skill development. Start with questions that are more mundane like what type of fruit or product to buy while grocery shopping. By practicing with questions that aren't very important, you will be more confident with your self-testing when you ask questions that are very important, especially during the Archangel Clearings Technique.

Chapter Seven
Members of the Spiritual Clearing Team

Since many of you may be unfamiliar with the specific Beings that assist with the Archangel Clearings, I will provide you with a very brief overview of who they are and how they are helping humanity. The following is a brief overview of the Dimensional Beings who will be called forth and perform the Archangel Clearings.

- **I AM Presence**

  This phenomena is an immortal Body of Light Substance that serves as the Presence of Source, which is the reality of who you are. If you were to see the Body of Light, it would appear in a form similar to the physical body, but vibrating at a much higher rate and therefore not visible to the naked eye.[40]

- **Lord Sananda**

  He was known on this planet as Jesus, but in other realms as Sananda, and serves as the World Teacher. He was one of the greatest Spiritual Healers that walked our precious planet Earth. He came to demonstrate how to achieve union with the Higher Self to become one with Source. He realigns, awakens, and heals the heart to the vibration of Unconditional Love.[41]

• **Mother Mary**

In all her incarnations, Mary worked closely with her twin flame, Archangel Raphael. He remained in the plane of Spirit (Heaven) to focus the energies of Alpha, while she remained on the plane of Matter (Earth) to focus the energies of Omega. In her final embodiment, she gave birth to Lord Jesus Christ.[42]

• **Kwan Yin**

Known as the Goddess of Mercy, Compassion, and Forgiveness, she is a member of the Karmic Board. Her service to humanity is Mercy and Healing. She is one of the Goddesses who are in charge of directing healing energy to the people of Earth. The name Kwan Yin (also spelled Kuan Yin, Quan Yin, Kuan Shih Yin), in Chinese roughly translates as "The One Who Hears the Cries of the World."[43]

• **Beloved Legions of Light**

These are Angels who are in service to this cause of eliminating negative energies from the planet.[44]

• **Master St. Germain**

He is the Lord of the Seventh Ray of Transmutation. The nature of the Seventh Ray is to purify the energy and substance of life. His gift to humanity is the Violet Transmuting Flame that can be invoked through the power of visualization, contemplation, intention, or by decree. It can be used to consume mistakes, remove negativity from self or environment, cleanse and purify your mind, and raise your vibrations.[45]

• **The Great White Brotherhood**

This Spiritual Order of Hierarchy is an organization of Ascended Masters united for the highest purposes of God in man as set forth by Lord Sananda and other World Teachers. The word "white" does not refer to race, but to the aura (halo) of the White Light that surrounds the saints and sages of all ages who have risen from every nation to be counted among the immortals.[46]

• **Angels of the Violet Fire**

These are the Angels of the Seventh Ray who purify everything whenever they pass by. There are Legions of these Violet Fire Angels. When summoned, they gather around you. With palms outstretched, they direct across your four lower bodies and your aura. As that arc flashes across your Being, it vaporizes the adverse conditions from your heart and mind.[47]

• **Archangel Michael**

He is known as the warrior Archangel that battles evil and cleanses people and places of discord and negativity. His color is blue, and he is the Archangel of Protection. He challenges humans who hold evil or harmful intentions to transmute them into positive and higher divine energies. His Flaming Blue Sword can be called upon to sever your self-imposed psychic ties to perceived limitations and attachments.[48]

• **Archangel Raphael**

He is known as the Archangel of Healing and the guardian of creative talents who brings happiness and joy. His color is green. He is charged with the sacred duty to heal the Earth and to heal humanity of its maladies. He assists during the healing process, mainly connected to psychic injuries.[49]

• **Archangel Uriel**

Known as the Archangel of Truth, he helps us with intellectual information, practical solutions, and creative insight. He transmutes all distortions connected with Truth, including lies, misuse of power, and energies connected with various forms of self-deception. His colors are ruby and gold.[50]

• **Archangel Gabriel**

Gabriel is known as the Archangel of Visitation. He transmutes all negative energies connected with love. He is the bringer of good news and a maker of changes who assists people with their spiritual purpose. His color is white, and his symbol is the lily.[51]

- **Archangel Chamuel**

  Chamuel is the Angel of Adoration. His service and outpouring is adoration to God, the angels, and all the powers that minister to humanity and the Earth. His color is pink, and his qualities are love, tolerance, and gratitude. His mission is to remind us to magnify the good.[52]

- **Archangel Jophiel**

  His service to life is in the teaching of the consciousness, enabling it to discover within itself the power of Light. He is the Archangel of Illumination. He encourages us to magnetize divine ideas, and within each plan is the way and means of fulfilling it. His color is yellow, and his qualities are wisdom, illumination, and perception.[53]

- **Archangel Zadkiel**

  Zadkiel, known as the Archangel of Mercy & Benevolence, helps us feel mercy and compassion toward ourselves and others. His color is violet, and he works closely with Ascended Master St. Germain and assists Archangel Michael when necessary in battling evil forces.[54]

- **Deva of the Earth Kingdom**

  The word "deva", from the Sanskrit language, means "a being of brilliant light", and is used to indicate a non-physical being. These are Nature Beings, similar to the Guardian Angels of humankind that exist in a parallel kingdom to humanity. Each deva has its specific area of responsibility to oversee. The devas are receptive and passive, and wait for instruction, as they are the feminine aspect.[55]

- **Deva of Healing**

  This Deva is a fifth-dimensional frequency and works quite closely with your Higher Self. The order, organization, and life vitality of the human body falls within the domain of the Deva of Healing.[56]

• **Pan and the Nature Spirits**

Pan is the heart energy that fine-tunes the frequencies between
the Elementals, Mother Earth and our vibrations by working with
the frequencies of Love and Light. Pan exists on a universal and
multidimensional level.[57]

• **Ancestors and Guardians of** (the area or property)

Often, the land receiving the Archangel Clearing was formerly in-
habited by ancestors, before the current owners. In many situations the original people were removed forcibly or in a violent
manner. By requesting the assistance of these Beings, the imprinted negative energies of these past actions can be released
from the confines of the Earth.

Chapter Eight
Divine Protection

You would not be reading this book unless you had embraced your spiritual side and wish to develop it more fully. As you advance on your spiritual journey, it is vital that you pray and ask for protection every day, as well as creating it for yourself. The security you ask for is from all forms of negativity. There is much negativity in the world at this time. As you bring forth more Light, darkness is drawn to it as if by a magnet. Make it a habit to place protection around yourself and your loved ones, diligently, twice a day. However; it would be ideal to request spiritual protection every morning upon arising; every afternoon; and before going to bed. If you do this consistently, the negative invasion can be averted.[58] I also recommend that you consider performing a weekly Archangel Clearing for yourself, as well.

First of all, it is essential to remember that fear always gives away your power. By maintaining a positive attitude and a sense of self, a person can often avoid negativity in most situations. Secondly, I suggest that you call upon Archangel Michael every day to place a golden dome of protection around you, especially upon awakening and, more importantly, before going to sleep. You can intercede many, many problems in your life by taking the time to do these simple spiritual exercises. It is when you get lazy and don't do them, that you become vulnerable. However, you are only a victim if you allow yourself to be one. If you own your power and create your protection, then, in truth, you don't need to be concerned.[59]

Tri-colored Force Field Daily Protection

As part of daily spiritual practice, visualize, or imagine, three protective, concentric circles around you to maximize your spiritual protection. These bubbles are blue (Divine Power), gold (Divine Wisdom), and pink (Divine Love). It only takes a few moments to do, and yet it is very powerful if done daily, especially before sleeping and before starting the day.

As a suggestion, the following is a prayer/intention that you can adapt to whatever variation is comfortable for you to say or visualize:

> *Dear Mother/Father, God or Source,*
>
> *Please surround me (and my home)* **with the blue bubble of Divine Power, the gold bubble of Divine Wisdom, and the pink bubble of Divine Love.**
>
> *Thank you*

Pillar of Light

Since we live now in the psychic realm, there are living, pulsating negative vibrations around us. These vibrations move like a whirlpool of energy emanating negativity. They are the causes and cores of centuries of disqualified energy by humanity, and it is essential that you start your day with protection, like the Pillar of Light.[60]

This protective pillar is a tube of pure Light substance, invisible to the ordinary sight, but able to be seen with inner vision. However, it is not hollow like a tube. Instead, it has light through it like a pillar—in, through, and around your physical body—with a radius of about three (or up to nine) feet. It is like a tube composed of fiery, opaque, white spiritual fire and is condensed at the outer edge, like a border, to make it impenetrable to anything not of the Light. It extends from above the head to below the feet, giving protection to both the inner bodies and the physical body. See, or imagine, it descending from your I AM Presence and extending feet in diameter, all around you and beneath your feet. Imagine it blocking all negative energy directed at you. Then see the tube filled with Violet Fire, its spiritual power freeing you from your worries and concerns.[61]

To invoke this Pillar of Light, state:

> *I call upon my I AM Presence to project, establish and intensify your protective Pillar of pure Light—in, through, and around me. Charged with your invincible protection, all-powerful and impenetrable, it keeps me insulated to everything not of the Light, and keeps it sustained. Thank you.*

No matter what responsibilities you have, throughout the day, you may be bombarded with other people's fears, negative thought forms, and excessive demands. How can you manage to stay centered and at peace in the midst of all that? Call forth The Pillar of Light to build powerful energy of protection around you. It can protect you from negative forces emanating from a person sitting next to you or even touching your physical body. Additionally, this technique can allow you to be disconnected from the mass consciousness thought forms in the atmosphere. These thought forms are a collection of thoughts that have been released by humanity (the collective) over the years, that attract additional, impressions of the same kind.

As an example, when a cataclysm occurs, there may be thought forms of fear released by thousands of people that are real energies. These energies remain in the atmosphere and become like a vast cloud of fear for people to experience until it is released. Certain places on the Earth have denser concentrations of these thought forms than others. Consider the Middle East and all that has historically transpired in that region. The lingering thought forms from those past situations can still affect the people who walk through that area today.

This Pillar of Light must be created each day anew before starting your routine. It is an extension of your I AM Presence that descends in answer to your call. This cylinder of shimmering White Light keeps out negative energy and seals in the Violet Flame, thus helping you maintain your connection to your I AM Presence. It protects you from the energies of hatred, jealousy, anger, and even being manipulated by others about the way you should be, think, or act. It will protect you from any imperfect thought forms that are floating in the atmosphere. If you start your day with this Pillar of Light, you can have that protection before any negativity comes toward you.[62]

Though it cannot be broken by external negative energy, it can dissipate if you withdraw your attention from your I AM Presence. It can also be temporarily torn if you allow yourself to become upset. Since the stressors of your day can distract you from maintaining a constant connection to your I AM Presence, it is best to give the following decree at the start of each day to re-establish this protective force field around you. Then, you can reinforce it by repeating the decree during various activities throughout your day, such as driving in your car, or while doing daily chores. Just focus on the image in your mind's eye.[63]

Visualize a sphere of white light around the threefold flame within the heart. See this globe of white fire expand and see yourself inside an imaginary world. Visualize the cosmic white-fire radiance around yourself. When saying the following mantra, repeat it aloud three times to be the most effective.

Pillar of Light Mantra

Beloved, I AM Presence bright,
Round me seal your Pillar of Light
Let it keep my Being free
From all discord sent to me.

Circle of Blue Flame

If added protection is needed, invoke the following:

I ask my I AM Presence to surround my Protective Pillar of Light with your Circle of Blue Flame, and provide whatever added protection is required. I thank you.

Then picture, or sense, this Circle of Blue Flame (about four inches thick) surrounding your Pillar of Light. This intention must also be established daily.[64]

The following two meditations for spiritual protection were created by one of my spiritual teachers, the late William Baldwin, Ph.D., who was a pioneer in the area of Spirit Releasement.

Inner Shrine Meditation

Sit in a chair with feet flat on the floor, your back straight, hands held out about twelve inches away, palms facing your Heart Center so energy will go towards self.

Then visualize a Violet Flame sweeping up through your feet, swirling through the lower bodies and bathing every cell with its cleansing, transmuting power. This visualization is a cleansing process to remove cloudiness or darkness and build the Inner Shrine. The Violet Flame vibrates at the highest ultraviolet spectrum of the color frequencies, just above what our physical eyes can perceive

It needs to be created every day to become a pure channel for Source.

- Now think of your Higher Self as a sun and visualize a Golden Light coming from this sun—like a star or flame over your head—entering through the top of your head.
- When the Light is steady and is seen, or felt, with the "inner eye," focus on the Heart Center and visualize the sparkling star as before. Now extend the Light, by thought, until you

feel the energy flow slowly through your body down to the feet. You may feel a tingle or warmth.

- Next, through your intention, bring the Light back up to the heart and expand it out to the Etheric Body, then the Emotional Body and then to the Mental Body—illuminating every atom.

- After cleansing and balancing the above bodies by the use of the Source Energy which flows into your crown and through your hands, fill your entire Being with bright Blue-White Light.

- This same Light will also be used to encircle your magnetic field, which is egg-shaped and will protect you from mass consciousness and evil thoughts directed toward you. The opening at the top will lead the Source Light to you and protect you from all darkness.[65]

Sealing Light Meditation

According to the late Dr. Baldwin, this meditation is the first step in self-protection. It is to be visualized first thing in the morning upon awakening, several times a day, and at bedtime. After some practice, the visualized Sealing Meditation becomes automatic. It is like a light that is always on.

- Visualize or imagine a brilliant point of Light that is deep within your chest area. This spark of Light is your connection with Source and is always there.

- See this Light expand into your whole body. Feel the Light energy flowing through your arms and out your hands, moving down your legs and out your feet, and then filling your head.

- Now imagine that the Light is expanding out past the boundaries of your body, outside your physical form.

- Notice it expanding out about an arm's length in front of you, an arm's length behind you, and an arm's length on either side of you, as high as you can reach above your head, and down beneath your feet.
- See and feel this Light now, lovingly surrounding you like a giant egg-shaped cocoon of Light.
- Sparkling through this cocoon of Light now, begin to imagine iridescent pieces of emerald green for healing, and shimmering pieces of rose pink for love.
- This cocoon of Light does not interfere with any outward expression or incoming experience of love.
- Repeat this Meditation of Light when you awaken and before you go to sleep.
- Also, repeat this meditation whenever you feel tired or unhappy.
- See and feel this shimmering cocoon of Light every time you breathe. Soon it will be with you permanently.[66]

Light Worker's Shield

The following is adapted from another one of my spiritual teachers, the late Erik Berglund.

I ask that a Light Worker's Shield be put in place around me now.

I ask that **blue** light stream within, around, and through my entire Being.

I ask that **gold** light stream within, around, and through my entire Being.

I ask that **pink** light stream within, around, and through my entire Being.

I ask that a **rainbow** of colors (red, orange, yellow, green, blue, indigo, and violet) swirl within, around, and through my entire Being.

I ask that **white** light stream within, around, and through my entire Being.

I ask that **gold** light stream within, around, and through my entire Being.

I ask that **blue** light form an exterior grid on the outside of this Shield.

I ask that **gold** light layer over the blue grid on the outside of this Shield.

I ask that **pink** light finalize and surround the entire outside of this Shield.

I now ask my Higher Self to weave an Infinity Symbol of shimmering White Light around everything and for the Universe to maximize this protection that has been created.

Archangel Michael Evocation

Here is another one of the prayers given to me by one of my spiritual teachers, the late Erik Berglund.

In the name of my I AM Presence of Source within, I call forth Archangel Michael

- – In front of me

- – In back of me

- – To the right of me

- – To the left of me

- Above me

- Beneath me

- Within me

- And outer me

- All about me

Let no one doubt me. I AM his love protecting here.

Emergency Conditions

Sometimes a situation will arise where you might feel spiritually vulnerable, or sense the presence of an entity. Often this might happen in the middle of the night during your sleep state. In this type of event, the following Universal Commands will be helpful:

1. *You do not belong here! I command you to disappear and cease to exist!*

State this command verbally three times.[67]

1. *Dissolve, consume, and transmute with the power of the Violet Fire into the Source of All That Is!*

State this command verbally three times.[68]

Then visualize <u>Silver</u> energy flowing down from above your head and radiating outward to form a protective shield, or belt of power, around your solar plexus area. Next, imagine a protective globe of <u>Gold</u> Light flowing from above your head and building a protective orb of energy on the outside of your auric field to shield you.[69]

If you still feel that you are spiritually unsafe, call for extra assistance from the Spiritual Clearing Team from the Archangel Clearings as follows:

I call forth the Spiritual Clearing Team

I call forth the Spiritual Clearing Team

I call forth the Spiritual Clearing Team

I command removal of whatever is interfering with my free will NOW!

Then there is no need to do anything further except to thank and release the Spiritual Clearing Team.

As you experience the shifting energies of these current times, you are empowered by the processes above, and prayers to enhance your reality dynamically by increasing your vibratory rate. In doing so daily, you are assisting with elevating the frequency of the planet.

Chapter Nine
Spiritual Fitness

Spiritual fitness is a precursor to spiritual growth, and spiritual growth is an ongoing process. Regardless of what stage of life you are experiencing, you can always find something to learn and grow as a person. However, growing on a spiritual level is not an easy task and certainly does not happen quickly. When it comes to spirituality on a spiritual level, you must make daily choices that reflect choosing growth versus stagnation.

When developing your spiritual side, it is important to increase your vibrations so that you can raise the quality of your soul's energy. This can be accomplished in many ways: getting in touch with nature regularly, reading inspirational books, daily meditation, praying often, listening to spiritual music, chanting, or watching spiritually-based podcasts. Frequent contact with angels or spirit guides of 100% pure Light will usually result in improvement in all phases of your life, quicker manifestations of your prayers, and in becoming a more open and loving person to others.

A committed daily spiritual practice can assist with the development of a healthy emotional balance. It is crucial to allow yourself some regular time to create serenity and compassion to make the right choices throughout the day. At first, it can be a small amount of time devoted to focus on inner peace. Consistency is vital to maintain the daily time to incorporate it as a life change. It is essential to know that there is not one specific way to meditate, pray, or communicate with your guides, teachers, and angels.

However, when you do anything from your heart with feeling, focus, and intention, it is always effective. Choosing to live only in the present moment will generate the most difference for you since change is an inside job.

As you become more conscious of your thoughts, you will realize how much time you have wasted. Much energy has been expended thinking about the past, worrying about the future, or focusing on negative aspects of yourself and others. Every single thought is creating an image in your energy field. Ideas that are charged with either positive or negative emotion create an even greater memory. If you are to change your life in a sustained positive direction, the primary area for concentration is the mental body. Your thoughts are controlling the mental body of your auric field, and you have the opportunity before every thought to continue with that thought or to change it. If a negative thought slips into your consciousness, immediately say "Cancel, Clear" to erase the impact of the thought and replace the energy of it with a positive one. Eventually, you can train your mind to be more positive. The following are ideas that you might choose to focus on daily for spiritual equilibrium:

1. Start your day with yoga.
2. Practice gratitude.
3. Clear your aura of unwanted influences.
4. Envelop yourself in a circle of protection.
5. Give thanks to your food before eating.
6. Chant a mantra
7. Ground yourself into the core of the earth.
8. Release the past.
9. Meditate
10. Disconnect cords of negativity from others.
11. Align your chakras.
12. Thump your thymus for 2 minutes.
13. Read an uplifting passage or book.
14. Practice forgiveness for yourself and others.
15. Eat certified organic and GMO-free foods.
16. Breathe the correct colors into your chakras.
17. Avoid toxic chemicals and cosmetics.

18. Get quality sleep.
19. Do breath work of any type.
20. Surround yourself with positive people.
21. Move your muscles.
22. Practice aromatherapy
23. Count your blessings daily upon arising.
24. Pay it forward.
25. Release what you are reluctant to let go.
26. Walk in the rainfall to cleanse your aura.
27. Eat your meals mindfully.
28. Remember to play.
29. Cleanse and recharge your chakras.
30. Absorb prana from the sun, trees, or earth.

All of the above suggestions can be utilized to increase your vibrations. Raising your vibrations assists in raising your consciousness. When your consciousness is raised, you begin tapping into higher level energies, and your purpose and spiritual gifts will appear.

There are several key results that raising your vibrations will provide for you. These include (but are not limited to):

- Self-empowerment
- Greater creativity
- Advanced spiritual growth
- Present moment living
- Increased sense of joy and lightness
- More open and loving to others
- Communication with higher spiritual levels
- Deeper faith
- Quicker manifestations
- Increased ability to cope with other people's emotions
- Stronger auric field

It is widely known that it takes thirty days to establish a habit, so it is essential to create a spiritual routine that you can easily incorporate into your lifestyle daily, so it won't be too overwhelming. Use whatever amount of time is available at first, but commit to a consistent time of day for your focus and intention. Gradually, you will choose to increase the allocated amount of time as you strive toward spiritual wholeness. With steady growth, you will have access to everything in the Universe.

Chapter Ten
Disconnecting From the Matrix

Everything that has been thought or felt has left its imprint somewhere in the psychic atmosphere. The psychic aura of the planet is a direct reflection of how humanity as a whole has felt and thought over hundreds of thousands of years. The main events that have affected our history in some way are war, hunger, sickness, disaster, and religion. All this energy has been absorbed into the collective psychic world or the mass consciousness.[70]

This mass consciousness, also called the collective consciousness, continues to absorb more "like" energy from each thought, feeling, and idea that resonates with that same vibration. A prime example is fear. That is a consciousness with billions of people giving energy to it in some form or another. It is believed by many that there is consciousness for every energetic dynamic that exists.[71]

In other words, when you are dealing with your patterns, energies, and emotions, you are also dealing with all the similar resonant energies floating around. When you are working on your issues, you are also working on the collective energy of humanity and are profoundly influenced by it. As you move through your life in this Earth School, you acquire many emotions, attitudes, beliefs, and energies that are embraced as your own but are not yours.

These energies can influence your values, your choices, and your experiences. They can challenge your faith and trust in the Universe. Eventually, an individual can accept these energies as his or her own. This situation occurs subtly over time and without realizing that these influences are being absorbed from the collective (mass) consciousness, and the Matrix that surrounds the planet. The accumulation of these stagnant energies thwarts any potential personal growth, success, or self-acceptance. Often these energies create a sense of hopelessness, futility, or despair until an individual decides consciously to take action and to move off of the emotional hamster-wheel. When you disconnect from this collective consciousness, you are released from the states of consciousness which exist in the lower realms.

The first step in any change is to develop an awareness that something needs to be different. I have been guided to remind you of that option. Merely acknowledging that your current life is not working for you as you would desire, can be the turning point for change. Unfortunately, this is not a simple task for most, as it requires some deep inner reflecting. Once there, you must accept that you have gotten off track with your soul's purpose. When this awareness evolves, it is time to create a strategy to facilitate your renewed life pattern.

Simply by your sincere desire and motivation to change, you can develop a more positive outlook that is aligned with your soul's mission in this incarnation. The doorway for your opportunity to shift is within yourself. The creation of new attitudes, beliefs, choices, values, and possibilities can be accomplished through daily meditation, creative visualization, prayers, yoga, or breathing exercises. For this new vision to be anchored into your current life, focus on some daily quietude to start your day with positivity and anticipation.

This positive transformation can be accomplished through gratitude, compassion, de-stressing your daily life, eating healthy foods, invoking spiritual protection for your family, paying attention to your thoughts, and avoiding disharmonious situations and energies from others. Primarily, this spiritual buoyancy can also occur when you choose to shift your consciousness out of the lower frequency where the old matrix of collective consciousness exists to a more favorable rate of manifestation.

The biggest obstacle to achieving this feat is by releasing yourself of the fearful emotions you are holding. Fear, particularly, limits you from seeing the available space for change. We all have an essential role here on Earth. Releasing the energy of the collective consciousness is one of our most critical spiritual missions.[72] The Universal Law of Resonance states: whatever you focus on becomes your reality.[73]

To release the collective (mass) consciousness of fear and to reclaim your power, you will need to take action. Turn off the television. Reduce time spent on social media. Choose to quit watching the news and crime shows. Don't watch horror movies or violence. Be aware of what you focus on while using the computer. Spend some time daily and connect with the elements of nature. Do your inner work, for every answer you need, can be found within. Send love to your body, your family, your friends, your enemies, and the Earth daily. When self-limiting beliefs surface in your awareness, you can imagine releasing them out of the top of your head just like black puffs of smoke. Once you eliminate fear, your dreams will be more tranquil and prophetic.

Deflecting the currents of fear, rage, and confusion in the collective consciousness of humanity requires that the energies of joy be invoked from the Soul. This energy appears as a pale golden color, similar to ginger ale, and contains sparkling, effervescent bubbles of energy. This energy is accessed by connecting with your Soul and stating, *"**The nature of the Soul is joy. As the Soul, I invoke the energies of joy**"*. Visualize these energies cascading down from your crown chakra. Then allow this sensation to permeate your entire aura.[74]

Lastly, consciously and with intention, choose to exit the Matrix from each lower vibration emotion you experience. Then you will become aware of whether it is your own emotion or whether you were connected to the collective clouds of the psychic world of feelings and thoughts. I was guided to create the following two-step disconnection from the Matrix statement.

Remember, it is your intention to exit the Matrix that is the most important. I recommend that you begin with the most intense negative emotion that is apparent in your life. Otherwise, you might want to start with what I consider the top twelve in no particular order:

Fear	Betrayal
Anger	Confusion
Guilt	Abandonment
Anxiety	Separation
Grief	Sorrow/Sadness
Helplessness	Jealousy

Matrix Statements
(Stated verbally)

Repeat each statement until you notice a shift in your body, breathing, or mood. It usually doesn't take more than ten repetitions. As the density lifts, it is common to become aware of the next emotion(s) to disconnect.

1. *"I choose to disconnect from the Matrix of* (state the emotion) *that surrounds the planet."*
   After the shift occurs, then state the following verbally:

   "Anywhere that (state the emotion) *was released from the Matrix that surrounds the planet, fill any openings with unconditional love and the Light of Source."*

2. *"I choose to disconnect all my ancestors (past, present, future), from the matrix of (state the emotion) that surrounds the planet."*
"**Wherever** (state the emotion) **was released from the Matrix that surrounds the planet, flood those areas with unconditional Love and the Light of Source.**"

Furthermore, being in a place of calm stillness in your heart while chaos ensues in others around you will allow you to emanate a balanced vibration that will affect those closest to you. The best way this feeling state can be achieved is by staying as stress-free as possible with a positive outlook and focusing on a great future. Join groups of like-minded individuals with common goals for singing, meditation, prayer, or chanting. Groups can be powerful.

Chapter Eleven
Earth Healings

The following meditations can be performed after you have completed all the usual steps for implementing an Archangel Clearing for a property. **However, they must only be performed while you are in the protection of the sacred Chamber of the Divine Council of Universes.**

1. **Healing for Mother Earth**
   Ask for the healing currents of all the Spiritual Beings of 100% pure Light whose presence you have evoked to flow into the Earth.

   First, visualize, imagine, or ask that these divine energies be directed into the core of Mother Earth. Ask for a balancing and harmonizing in the foundation of the planet. Ask that Unconditional Love pour forth so that all that needs healing will be healed, balanced, and cleansed through Grace rather than karma. Ask the Archangels present to radiate their healing energies to the area surrounding the Earth. When finished, end the Meditation as you would complete an Archangel Clearing (expressing gratitude and then grounding yourself).[75]

2. **Diffusing Political Conflicts**
   Hold in your mind's eye and your heart, the specific political hot spot you have chosen. Evoke Master St. Germain to blaze the full-

gathered momentum of the Violet Transmuting Flame within, around, and through, that particular area to transmute all negativity. Ask the Archangels who are present to co-create a peaceful and harmonious situation. Call upon the Deva of that country or geographical area to offer her assistance there on an ongoing basis. When finished, end the Meditation as you would complete an Archangel Clearing (expressing gratitude and then grounding yourself).[76]

3. Eradicating Social Issues

Chose a specific social issue to which you feel closely attuned. Examples might be:

- religious intolerance
- racial strife
- children in need of greater protection
- human trafficking
- starving people
- refugees
- elevating the consciousness of youth or government officials
- elimination of domestic or child abuse
- the pervasive issue of homelessness

There is no end to the matters you might choose to focus on at this time in history.

Place your attention on the social issue you have selected as your world-service meditation and ask the Archangels present to channel Love and Light directly into the core of that issue. Visualize, imagine, or intend that the energy of the issue transforms from a situation of unfairness, disharmony, and discrimination into a Love-infused, Light-infused expression of Source. Call forth Master St. Germain to blaze the situation with the Violet Transmuting Flame to uplift and transform; that all may come into the highest expression of Source at any given time. When finished, end the Meditation as you would complete an Archangel Clearing (expressing gratitude and then grounding yourself).[77]

4. Preserving the Rainforests and all Other Forests

Ask the Archangels who are present and the Deva of the Rainforests and all other forests, to assist in building a group thought form strong enough to affect the thought forms of those who act to destroy these sacred lands.

Visualize, imagine, or intend that these forests are thriving and functioning in a beautiful harmony with humanity, and all the various kingdoms of evolution on this planet that help maintain the growth of all the forests. When finished, end the Meditation as you would complete an Archangel Clearing (expressing gratitude and then grounding yourself).[78]

5. Protecting Endangered Species and Other Animals

Ask the Archangels who are present and the Deva of the Animal Kingdom and all other animals to protect the endangered species of our world, help to cease animal abuse of every kind; and in its place, promote the compassionate treatment of the animal kingdom.

Visualize, imagine, or intend that animals of the wild rove freely about, following their instincts without interference from humanity; and that all forests and jungles are free and clear of any traps that could potentially harm these animals. Ask that alternatives be printed on the collective consciousness of humanity that will allow the cessation of animal experimentation, replaced by benign forms of study. When finished, end the Meditation as you would complete an Archangel Clearing (expressing gratitude and then grounding yourself).[79]

6. Preserving the Oceans and all Other Bodies of Water

Ask the Archangels who are present and the Deva of the Oceans and all its freshwater sources to assist in building a group thought form strong enough to affect the thought forms of those who act to destroy these pristine water resources.

Visualize, imagine, or intend that these oceans are thriving and functioning in a beautiful harmony with humanity, and all the various kingdoms of evolution on this planet that help maintain the purity of all the oceans and natural water sources. When finished, end the Meditation as you would complete an Archangel Clearing (expressing gratitude and then grounding yourself).[80]

7. Liberating Earthbound Souls

Many times the people who died in painful tragedies in the past are still Earthbound. They become trapped in time in the matter realms of the Earth and are unable to evolve their spirit into a future timeline. Ask the Archangels who are present to help awaken any souls that are trapped within the lower astral realms and are tied or held to the Earth in an unhealthy manner. Then they may willingly let go of all attachments that no longer serve them, and be assisted in making their full transition to the inner planes to continue their evolution.

Visualize, imagine, or intend that any negativity or emotionalism these earthbound souls may have unknowingly taken in, can now be removed so they can find their higher purpose within the Light. When finished, end the Meditation as you would complete an Archangel Clearing (expressing gratitude and then grounding yourself).[81]

8. Assisting Transitioning Souls

Ask the Archangels who are present to help any person or animal (*insert a specific person's or animal's name*) who is now going through their transition called death to move quickly, gently, and easily and to seek

only the highest Light. Ask that their lives on the inner plane be filled
with love, peace, and joy and that Light embraces them and calls them
Home as they merge with the Light of Source.[82]

Chapter Twelve
Glossary of Definitions

I received the following definitions from my many meditations over three decades of experiencing, and then releasing each that is listed. There is no reference source other than my Higher Self.

Glossary of Category Definitions

Accumulated Negative Energies: Grid-work that is created from long-standing negativity and stress can resemble a cage. This can create blockages to clarity, creativity, and cash flow.

Arch Demons: They understand only the negative energy of the lower three chakras: survival, fear, and control. They are extremely hostile, arrogant, and egotistical.

Astral Influences: These energies Interfere with the magnetic system of the body.

Auric Weaknesses: These holes, tears, fissures, and cracks are found in any layer of the human aura. They create vulnerability to negative energy attachments, and are caused by drugs, alcohol, trauma, intense emotions, and anesthesia. Also, they can be associated with past-life experiences.

Auric Webbing: This is comprised of layers of energy between auric bodies that disrupt the energy flow between levels of the aura.

Bondage: Primarily thought forms created to induce a sense of confusion. Also, it can cause addiction to a substance. Ethereally, these resemble ropes and chains.

Codes: Unique formatting imprinted into the mental body from a past life. They are connected to past-life karma.

Curse: A negative decree that is spoken aloud to evoke evil, strife, and harm upon someone or something. The curse may be from the past or the present. The general themes include love, money, health, and personal limitation.

Dark Angel: This category is another example of the dark force hierarchy. They attempt to deceive and influence spiritual seekers who do not qualify the source of their spiritual communication.

Demonic Presences: A low vibration and intelligence that has no soul and has never incarnated in its own human body. They thrive on the pain of human suffering and interfere with love relationships. They can induce self-destruction through undermining self-esteem.

Discarnate Souls: Deceased individuals who remain Earthbound by their own free- will after death. They retain their previous fears, emotions, interests, and attitudes. Often their physical body imprints are overlaid on the host's body, which may cause physical/emotional conditions or symptoms. May have addictions they wish to satisfy vicariously through the host.

Electromagnetic Interferences: These are types of vibratory barriers that disrupt the healthy equilibrium of the electromagnetic currents in the physical body, on any level.

Emotions: They are feeling states that have been created by events and people that individuals interface with in the course of a lifetime.

Encased Life Energies: These are rigid energetic encasements that protect the individual from any type of deep emotional feeling state. These can act as an energetic entrapment.

Energy Bands: Energy force fields, attached to the aura, which interfere with an individual's ability to communicate with higher spiritual beings. Can cause real headaches.

Energy cords: Energetic attachments to people, places, and things. They create an energy drain for an individual physically, mentally, and spiritually and keep people "stuck" and possessions from selling. Often, these occur when people give their power away to others.

Energy implants: Energy plugs implanted in chakras or aura intentionally. Usually, these are composed of astral substances.

False Beliefs: These are beliefs based on a person's perception rather than Truth.

Fakers: This category pretends to be our Higher Self. Common in spiritually awake people.

Force Fields: Negative vibration barrier that surrounds people or places and buffers access to higher vibrational energies. Can disrupt energy flow from upper to lower chakras and hold people trapped in negativity.

Fragmented Souls: These are splinters or parts of self or other souls, created by traumatic events.

Frequency Controls: Rates of vibrations that enter the energy field for programming purposes and to manipulate thinking. Can cause fear and anxiety.

Highly Evolved Dark Masters: Ascended Beings that have chosen to serve the advancement of humankind by attempting to draw human souls away from their spiritual path and life's purpose. They screen out the souls whose dedication, wisdom and insight are not developed enough to allow them to advance to higher spiritual realms.

Inner Conflicts: Often these Internal struggles concern one's beliefs, attitudes, desires, abilities, and emotions. Keeps one immobilized as to what is the right action. These are frequently created from fear and guilt.

Inner shadow: Negative energy outside the body that slides in between a person and his or her Higher Self, to block information of a spiritual nature and discourages meditations.

Interferences with Cash Flow: Energetic blockages to the receipt and flow of money to people, personally, and to businesses. Can paralyze self by thinking negatively about money.

Interferences with Thoughts: Mental turbulence projected from an outside energetic source to reduce focus and clarity.

Killer Psychic Energies: Negative energies that are directed toward anyone who contemplates raising his or her consciousness. They attempt to weaken and gain entry into the person's life force energy. These energies often keep someone from falling asleep when exhausted.

Locks: Self-imposed energetic blockages to the chakras or between auric layers. The intention is to shut down emotions to cope effectively with life situations. These obstruct the electromagnetic flow of energy through the chakras.

Manipulations: Distractions, obstacles, and delays connected to spiritual situations, careers, and relationships, often to throw people off their path.

Mass Consciousness: This term refers to the singular identity of a group and its beliefs. It is also referred to as "the collective" as it is the recorded collective memory of the planet.

Members of the Dark Brotherhood: Negative forces that seek to hinder the spiritual advancement of humanity. They cause difficulties for individuals, create confusion about spirituality, and sidetrack people's energies.

Negative Energizer: Functions like a battery to feed any negativity a person encounters.

Negative Essences: These are the heavy residues left from an accumulation of negative thought forms or any other type of negativity.

Negative High Levels: Negative forces have a hierarchy in dark consciousness, as do spiritual beings ascending to the Light. Their original intent is to detour seekers from their path.

Negative Thought forms: Creations of human thought that remain hovering around a person or geographic location, developed over centuries from people practicing evil intent. Can resemble a cloud. Also, they can be projected by outside forces.

Open Psychic Door: The Psychic door is located at the base of the skull. This door should be kept closed and guarded by a gatekeeper.

Overshadow: Negative energy outside the body that slides in between a person's Higher Self and "All That Is." Hinders the creation of a secure God connection.

Past Life Binds: These are contracts, agreements, or karma that are carried over from previous lifetimes and impede spiritual progress. Often people continue to repeat patterns and lessons until these are removed.

Prejudices: These are preconceived judgments or opinions that are usually unfavorable. They are often unjustified and unreasonable biases.

Programming: Directed messages telepathically imprinted in the mental body of the aura by outside energy or force.

Psychic Bonding: It is an unhealthy, obsessive or emotional attachment to something with inability to let go.

Psychic Shocks to Chakras & Auras: Projected assaults on an individual's energy centers to keep a person off balance, fatigued, disoriented, or ungrounded.

Psychic Vampire: A person who magnetizes energy away from another person's auric field. Usually, this is a weak individual who draws strength from someone stronger. Can also be an unhealthy parent living off his or her child's vitality.

Residents: Types of discarnates that are energetically attached inside one of the auric layers. They sap strength and distort mental perspective. They function as a partial possession.

Satanic Energies: These are very dark energies that attempt to draw human souls away from their spiritual purpose. They do not believe in the reality of Christ and the validity of His message.

Self-inflicted Thought forms: These self-imposed beliefs and inner truths stem from childhood memories, past traumas, or lack of forgiveness of self.

Telepathic Pathways: Negative information and energies that are not being channeled for the highest good.

Unnamed negative energies: All categories that are not listed or known at this time.

Vibrational Influences: These currents of energy interfere with and manipulate the normal electromagnetic flow of the subtle bodies.

Conclusion

As we walk the path we have chosen in this Earth sojourn, we want to assure that we make a difference for having been here, no matter how small the legacy. Each of us is a viable piece in a grand puzzle of the evolution of humanity. When we change our inner world, the world outside can change as a result.

This is an auspicious time in the evolution of the planet. Don't be distracted and miss the chance to include your contributions to a better world. The time for change is now, so take that first step!

Acknowledgments

It is with the deepest of gratitude that I thank the following for assisting me with the creation of this third book: All my Guides and Teachers of 100% pure Light; the Archangels and the Ascended Masters; and the Beings of Light from the Spiritual Clearing Team for their love, guidance, and inspiration.

I want to express sincere gratitude to the following for their contributions in developing this book: Dr. David Bone, Paula Snellings and Connie Repoli for their enthusiasm and support and The Sisters of Notre Dame at the LIAL Renewal Center for providing the conditions I needed to write this book. I deeply appreciate and thank the following published authors: Diane Wing, Ray Sette, Amara Mahdhuri and Carol May for reading the manuscript and providing a review of the book. I would also like to express gratefulness to all who have sponsored and attended my Weekend Intensives for their contributions, experiences, and valuable feedback.

My heartfelt thanks and gratitude also goes to the following individuals: my sister, Kristy for her unconditional love and support all along the way; my daughters Kimberly and Kelley and my grandchildren Avery and Quinn, who have allowed me to love fully. I also wish to extend many blessings to the following: all past, present, and future students and clients; all who have assisted me, both known and unknown, on my spiritual journey; and all who read this book and use the information to improve the quality of their life on their spiritual path.

About the Author
Rev. Diana Burney, RN, BSN, M.Ed., D.D.

Diana has over 40 years' experience in management, counseling, marketing, and education. She developed successful private counseling practices in four states while remaining current with appropriate credentials for the health care arena. Diana is a registered nurse, certified hypnotherapist and ordained minister of the Order of Melchizedek from the Sanctuary of the Beloved in Conesus, New York. She is also a certified Reiki Master/Teacher as well as a Magnified Healing Practitioner. She holds a Master's in Education from Cleveland State University and a Doctorate of Divinity degree from The College of Divine Metaphysics in Glendora, California. Diana has done hundreds of thousands of Archangel Clearings for properties, individuals, and animals over the past 28 years. These Archangel Clearings have been done in every state in the US and over 80 foreign countries. Without advertising these services, individuals have found her after hearing about the phenomenal success of the work she has done. She has been featured in SPA magazine, and articles have been written in the Toronto Star and the Florida-Times Union about her success with remote Energy Clearings for homes and property.

Diana has appeared on various cable TV, and radio shows including Coast to Coast with Art Bell and the Uri Geller Show. She has been teaching Spiritual Clearing Weekend Intensives for over twenty years, five of those years at Fellowship of the Spirits in Cassadaga, NY. Also, she is the author of two award-winning books, *Spiritual Clearings* and *Spiritual Balancing.* She currently lives in Ann Arbor, MI and has been the President of Earth Release since 1999 and Founder of Healing Vibrations since 2001. She is available for speaking engagements, interviews, and appearances. She can be reached through her Earth Release website: www.earthrelease.com

End Notes

[1] Source Unknown

[2] Burney, Diana. *Spiritual Clearings: Sacred Practices to Release Negative Energy and Harmonize Your Life*: Berkeley: North Atlantic Books, 2009.

[3] Stone, Joshua David. *Soul Psychology: How to clear Negative Emotions and Spiritualize your life*. New York: Ballantine Wellspring, Ballantine Pub. Group, 1999, Pg. 285.

[4] Starr, Aloa. *Prisoners of Earth: Psychic Possession and Its Release*. Arizona: Light Technology Publishing, 1987, Pg. 44.

[5] https://www.wongkiewkit.com/forum/ Author Unknown, 2005.

[6] Source Unknown

[7] http://www.unity.org/resources/articles/prayer-protection.

[8] Mitchell, Wayne. *New Heart English Bible*. (Bloomington, IN: Authorhouse, 2008), Mathew 6:9-13.

[9] Crowley, Brian & Esther. *Words of Power: Sacred Sounds of East & West*. Llewellyn Publications. (St. Paul, Minnesota, 1991) Pgs.65-68.

[10] Chanera. *"I AM" Adorations and Affirmations: Part I*. (Schaumburg. IL: Saint Germain Press INC, 1993), Pg. 3.

[11] Crowley, 159-161.

[12] Crowley, 163-166.

[13] Truman, Karol K. *Feelings Buried Alive Never Die …* (Las Vegas, NV: Olympus Distributing,1991) Pgs. 220-264.

[14] Judith, Anodea. *Wheels of Life: A User's Guide to the Chakra System*. Llewellyn Publications. (St. Paul, Minnesota, 1988) Pgs.46-47.

[15] Jasmuheen. *In Resonance* Self-Empowerment Academy (Kenmore, Australia, 1996) Pgs. 33-34.

[16] Source Unknown

17 https://www.wongkiewkit.com/forum/forum/suggested-reading/articles-and-popular-topics/2938-heal-yourself-before-healing-others.

[18] http://www.unity.org/resources/articles/prayer-protection

[19] Mitchell, Wayne. *New Heart English Bible.* (Bloomington, IN: Authorhouse, 2008), Mathew 6:9-13.

[20] Crowley, Brian & Esther. *Words of Power: Sacred Sounds of East & West.* Llewellyn Publications. (St. Paul, Minnesota, 1991) Pgs. 65-68.

[21] Chanera. *"I AM" Adorations and Affirmations: Part I.* (Schaumburg. IL: Saint Germain Press INC, 1993), Pg. 3.

[22] Crowley, 159-161.

[23] Crowley, 163-166.

[24] Source Unknown

[25] https://www.learnreligions.com/st-Francis-of-Assisi-patron-saint-124533

[26] https://discoveringdowsing.com

[27] Mitchell, Karyn K. Reiki: Beyond the Usui System, Pg. 222.

[28] Jurriaanse, D. *The Practical Pendulum Book,* York Beach, Maine (Samuel Weiser, INC, 1986) Pgs. 1-3.

[29] Olson, Dale. *The Pendulum Charts,* (Eugene, OR Crystalline Publications, 1989) Pgs. 1-2.

[30] Wright, Machelle Small. *M.A.P. Medical Assistance Program.* (City, Publisher), Date, Pgs. 243-245.

31 https://discoveringdowsing.com/finger-thumb_dowsing

32 www.beyond-hearing-voices.com

33 https://www.perelandra-ltd.com/PKTT-Self-Testing-Steps-W75.aspx.

34 https://www.livestrong.com/article/325815-techniques-for-self-
muscletesting

35 https://hblu.org/self-help-information/muscle-testing-self-help-
techniques.html

36 www.angelguides.com/how-to-muscle-test-yourself.

37 Doering, Julie Renee. *Your Divine Blueprint,* (Gable Kennedy-Middletown,
DE, 2015), Pg. 245.

38 https://discoveringdowsing.com/3-favorite-deviceless-
dowsingtechniques

39 Prophet, Elizabeth Clare, and Patricia R. Spadaro. *Alchemy of the Heart:
How to Give and Receive More Love.* (Corwin Springs, MT: Summit
University Press, 2000), pg. 128.

40 Printz, Thomas. *The Seven Mighty Elohim Speak on the Seven Steps to
Precipitation.* (Mount Shasta, CA: Ascended Master Teaching
Foundation,1986),Pg. 29.

41 Cooper, Diana. *A New Light on Ascension,*(Scotland, UK: Findhorn Press,
2002), pg.144.

42 Cooper, pg. 145.

43 Virtue, Doreen, PhD. *Archangels & Ascended Masters* (Carlsbad, CA:Hay
House, ,2003), pg. 98.

44 Schroeder, Werner, *The Angelic Kingdom,* (Mount Shasta, CA: Ascended
Master Teaching Foundation, 2008), pg.45-35.

45 Virtue, pg. 153-155.

46 Virtue, pg. 233.

47 Schroeder, pg.13.

48 Cooper, Diana and Whild, Tim. *The Archangel Guide to Ascension,*(Carlsbad,
CA: Hay House, 2015) pg.118-120.

[49] Virtue, pg. 38-30.

[50] Virtue, pg. 45.

[51] Virtue, pg. 21.

[52] Virtue, pg.19.

[53] Schneider, Petra and Pieroth, Gerhard, *Archangels and Earthangels*, (Twin Lakes, WI, Arcana Publishing, 2000), pg. 118-119.

[54] Schneider and Pieroth, pg. 124-125.

[55] Shumsky, Susan, *Ascension: Connecting with the Immortal Masters and Beings of Light,* (Franklin Lakes, NJ, 2010) pg.59.

[56] Hummel, Christan, *Space Clearing Kit,* (Oceanside, CA:One Source Publications 2004), pg, 120.

[57] www.crystallinks.com/nature_spirits.html.

[58] Stone, Joshua David. *Soul psychology: How to Clear Negative Emotions and Spiritualize Your Life.* New York: Ballantine Wellspring, Ballantine Pub. Group, 1999, Pg. 280.

[59] Stone, Joshua David. *Beyond Ascension: How to Complete the Seven Levels of Initiation.* Sedona, AZ: Light Technology Pub., 1995, pg. 99.

[60] Printz, Thomas. *The Seven Mighty Elohim Speak on the Seven Steps to Precipitation.* Mount Shasta, Calif. Ascended Master Teaching Foundation, 1986. Pg. 28 Pg. 92, I AM Guard, Prophet.

[61] Printz, Thomas. *The Seven Mighty Elohim Speak on the Seven Steps to Precipitation.* Mount Shasta, Calif. (P.O. Box 466, Mount Shasta 96067): Ascended Master Teaching Foundation, 1986. Pg. 28.

[62] Prophet, Elizabeth Clare. *Access the Power of Your Higher Self.* Corwin Springs, Mont.: Summit University Press, 1997.pg. 48

[63] Luk, A.D.K. *The Law of Life: Book II,* (Pueblo, Colorado: A.D.K. Luk Publications, 1989), Pg. 37.

[64] Prophet, pg. 49.

[65] Baldwin, William J. *Healing Lost Souls: Releasing Unwanted Spirits from Your Energy Body.* (Charlottesville, VA: Hampton Roads Pub)., 2003, Pg. 273.

[66] Baldwin, William J. *Spirit Releasement Therapy: A Technique Manual.* (Terra Alta, WV: Headline Books, 1992), Pg. 385.

[67] Luk, A.D.K. *The Law of Life: Book II,* (Pueblo, Colorado: A.D.K. Luk Publications, 1989) pg. 37 Law of Life.

[68] Starr, Aloa, *Prisoners of Earth: Psychic Possession and Its Release* (Sedona, AZ: Light Technology Publishing, 1993, pg.164.

[69] Two Disciples. *The Rainbow Bridge* (Danville, CA: Rainbow Bridge Productions,1982), 189.

[70] Ken Page and Nancy Nester. *Energy Techniques for Spirit Releasement,* (Cleveland, GA: Clear Light Arts, ADL, 2004), pg. 70.

[71] Bloom, William. *Psychic Protection.* (Piatkus Pub., 2012), pg. 134-135.

[72] Page and Nester, pg. 71.

[73] https:lawsoftheuniverse.weebly.com/law-of-resonance.html.

[74] Two Disciples, pg. 189.

[75] Stone, Joshua David. *How to Teach Ascension Classes* (Sedona, AZ: Light Technology Pub., 1998), pg. 57.

[76] Adapted from Stone, pg. 58.

[77] Adapted from Stone, pg. 59.

[78] Adapted from Stone, pg. 67.

[79] Adapted from Stone, pg. 73.

[80] Adapted from Stone, pg. 68.

[81] Adapted from Stone, pg. 62.

[82] Adapted from Stone, pg. 61.

Made in the USA
Las Vegas, NV
10 January 2022

40948397R00080